# ADVERSITY IS MY ANGEL

## THE LIFE AND CAREER OF
## RAÚL H. CASTRO

# ADVERSITY IS MY ANGEL

## THE LIFE AND CAREER OF
## RAÚL H. CASTRO

## RAÚL H. CASTRO AND
## JACK L. AUGUST, JR.

TCU PRESS
FORT WORTH, TEXAS

Library of Congress Cataloging-in-Publication Data

Castro, Raúl H., 1916-
Adversity is my angel : the life and career of Raúl H. Castro / Raúl H. Castro and
Jack L. August, Jr.
p. cm.
Includes bibliographical references and index.
ISBN 978-0-87565-378-5 (pbk. : alk. paper)
1. Castro, Raúl H., 1916- 2. Governors--Arizona--Biography. 3. Ambassadors--
United States--Biography. 4. Hispanic Americans--Arizona--Biography. I. August,
Jack L. II. Title.
F815.3.C37A3 2009
327.730092--dc22
[B]
2008044533


TCU Press
P. O. Box 298300
Fort Worth, Texas 76129
817.257.7822
http://www.prs.tcu.edu
To order books: 800.826.8911


Designed by Vicki Whistler

# CONTENTS

cﬂ

# INTRODUCTION

⚕

Raúl H. Castro's unlikely but distinguished professional career suggests the adversity inherent in his humble beginnings only hardened his resolve and strengthened his determination. He was born into grinding poverty and minority status on the US–Mexico border, but eventually overcame those obstacles to become, among other titles, Arizona's first Hispanic governor. Castro's story, which suggests much about the human spirit and the hope of the American Dream, is one that ought to be told. [1]

In December of 2000 Henry Zipf and Ben Williams Jr., longtime friends of Castro, met to discuss the possibilities of writing his memoir. The men hoped to explore his remarkable memory by conducting a series of interviews with Castro. Their goal: the preservation of the full and rich memories from a varied and interesting life and illustrious career.

Some of Castro's earliest memories were of his poor immigrant mother sending him into the southern Arizona desert to collect cactus fruit to feed the family. During his childhood, he experienced racial prejudice, demeaning comments, and heard repeatedly that he would spend his life in the southern Arizona copper mines. Castro's childhood serves as a metaphor for Mexican and American attitudes of mutual suspicion and distrust along the US–Mexico border.

Yet, in spite of such a disadvantaged beginning, Castro found a way to get an education and embark on his path to the prominent position he holds today, beginning as a teacher, then a lawyer, then Pima County attorney, superior court judge of Pima County, the governor of Arizona, and American ambassador to El Salvador, Bolivia, and Argentina. Though Castro suffered innumerable instances of social and racial discrimination, he overcame institutional and personal prejudice to attain the livelihood he desired. Raúl Castro's life and career serve as dual role models, not only to Mexican Americans, but to all Americans. [2]

# CHAPTER I

## ANCESTORS AND IMMIGRANTS

My father was born and grew up in a small fishing village near the tip of the Mexican state of Baja California, called San José del Cabo. He was of Basque-Mexican origin, and most of the Basque male inhabitants were over six feet tall and came from Spain, so they had the unique characteristic of being taller than most Mexicans. Like the other Basques, my father was tall, about six foot two, and weighed about two hundred and forty pounds. He was a big man; not fat, but husky, and all muscle. He was a good swimmer, and as a young man he worked as a pearl diver for companies, retrieving pearls from oysters. As a result, he never went to school.

When he was a young man he moved about halfway up the Baja peninsula to the little town of Santa Rosalía, which is across from Guaymas on the mainland. There he met my mother, Rosario Acosta, who, like most Mexican women in the area, had a good deal of Indian blood in her. They fell in love and were married. My mother only made it through the third grade, but with that she was able to teach my father to read.[1]

My father's name in Mexico was Francisco Castro Dominguez. As is the custom in Spanish-speaking countries, Francisco was his given name, Castro was his father's surname, and Dominguez was his mother's surname. In Mexico people called him Señor Castro or Señor Castro Dominguez. But later, when he immigrated to the United States, the family adopted the American custom of placing the father's surname last, and his name became Francisco D. Castro. When I was born, my name became Raúl Castro. However, when I graduated from high school in Douglas, Arizona, a line formed in the principal's office so he could get the correct full name of each graduate to put on the diplomas. All of the Anglo students had middle names. I had no middle name, and I wanted to be like them, so I chose the first name of a local basketball player in Douglas whom I admired, Hector Miranda. I told the principal my full name was Raúl Hector Castro. I just made it up, and since then it has always been with me. I often wish I had chosen a better name.

The French influence from the days of Maximilian I and his intervention in Mexico (1864-1867) persisted in Santa Rosalía. French was the second language used among the citizenry, and more than a few elites remained in the community. In fact, the French dominated the local economy; they owned and operated the local smelter, El Boleo, which was the major employer. As it turned out, Santa Rosalía provided few economic opportunities for my parents. Even though my mother was born there, the family decided to move to the mainland—to Guaymas, Sonora.[2] They sailed across the Gulf of California, a trip that took seven days due to storms and rough seas. My mother claimed she feared for her life, but the family needed to broaden their economic horizons.[3]

The move to the port city of Guaymas proved temporary. Soon my father and mother heard that new jobs were available to the north in the smelter and mines of an emerging mining empire in Cananea, Sonora. Colonel William Cornell Greene—a powerful and colorful cattle baron, copper mine owner, and self-promoter in Cochise County on the Arizona side of the border—owned the Cananea Consolidated Copper Company, or the "Four Cs." Cananea lies thirty miles south of the Arizona border, about halfway between Nogales, Arizona, and Douglas, Arizona. Not surprisingly, Greene exploited the Mexican workforce. Conditions and wages were terrible, but fortunately my father, who now had eight children to feed, found jobs in both the smelter and in the American-owned mines in 1914.[4]

Due to the exploitation and dreadful employment practices, my father became involved in the miners' union, called Sindicato Sesenta y Cinco (Union Sixty-Five). My father became a union leader and took part in setting up an unsuccessful strike. Greene responded by labeling my father a "rabble-rouser," and he convinced the Mexican authorities to arrest and jail him at the capital in Hermosillo.[5]

My father spent six months in prison, and after several efforts to free him my sister, Enriqueta, smuggled crucial information to him.[6] As an upshot of this and other entreaties, the Mexican government agreed to an amnesty and political asylum. Ironically they released my father from prison on the condition that he left Mexico. The entire family immigrated to the United States, to the little town of Pirtleville, Arizona, about four miles northwest of Douglas.

In early 1918 my family crossed the border at Naco, about fifteen miles south of Bisbee, in Cochise County, Arizona. By now my parents had eleven children, and we entered a new country with different customs and a different language. The immigration officer looked at us and said, "Castro family, you are now in the United States of America. The rest is up to you."[7] It was up to us. So we went to work.

My father found work in the smelter in Douglas. The town was named after mining pioneer James Douglas and was founded as a smelter town to treat the copper ores of nearby Bisbee, Arizona. Two copper smelters operated at the site: the Calumet and Arizona Company Smelter, built in 1902, and the Copper Queen operated in Douglas from 1904–1931, when Phelps Dodge Corporation purchased the Calumet and Arizona Company and took over their smelter. The Calumet and Arizona smelter became the Douglas Reduction Works.[8]

My father, upon bringing his family to the United States, enabled us to make an important choice. The leaders of the small but growing Mexican community in Pirtleville wanted him to register all of us as Mexican citizens.[9] He refused and added that we deserved to make our own choices as to whether we wanted to register as either Mexican or American citizens. Ten Castro children lived to adulthood, nine boys and one girl. The birth order was Ramón, Enriqueta, Isidoro, Francisco, Angel, Ignacio, Alfonso, myself, Ernesto, and Romero. I was born on June 12, 1916, in Cananea, Sonora, Mexico.[10] While Pirtleville framed my childhood memories, on occasion my mother took us for extended visits to Cananea, Mexico, so I grew up in an international and border-regional context.

Anglo American mine owners established Pirtleville as a company town for the Mexican smelter workers. About two thousand people lived in the town, and only three Anglo families lived among us. The Balich and Herolich families hailed from Yugoslavia and the Corvallos were Italian. All worked, attended school, played together and, not surprisingly, spoke Spanish like natives of Mexico. Schools in Pirtleville and Douglas was segregated; Mexican children went to the Fifteenth Street School or the Seventh Street School in Douglas.[11] I went to the Fifteenth Street School, and then the Seventh Street School until about the sixth grade. The Dunbar School on F Avenue was for African American children, and the two other elementary schools in Douglas, the A Avenue School and the Clawson School, were for Anglo students.

We walked four miles to school each morning from Pirtleville to Douglas and the four miles back again in the afternoon. The Douglas school system ran a bus to the perimeter of Pirtleville and the surrounding areas each morning and picked up the Anglo children. They rode to Douglas, but the Mexican children walked. The bus passed us on the dirt road, and our Anglo friends waved, but the bus driver never offered us a ride. I knew this practice was an injustice.

In the late teens and early twenties my father worked on the Bull Gang, which lifted and moved heavy objects in the smelter. They used a crane to do steelwork, yardwork, and related tasks, and without a union the most he took home was $3.20 a day. He died prematurely from pneumonia at forty-three years of age.[12]

The copper smelting process was arduous, time consuming, and labor intensive. First a train transferred raw ore from the Bisbee, Ajo, and Nacozari mines. The ore was crushed and transferred to the roaster building on a conveyor belt. The workmen, using natural gas, heated the ore to about 1200° F, and after that process they took the ore to the reverbatories and uniformly distributed the ore and then smelted it at about 2400° F. This produced two materials: the waste, or "slag," which rose to the top, and the heavier "matt" material, composed mostly of copper metal along with some gold and silver, which settled at the bottom. My father, and other workers like him, skimmed the slag off the top, and took the matt to the converter. Here the matt, exposed to air blown at a very high pressure, became a charge of copper. My father and his co-workers then took the charge of copper to the anode machines and poured it into bars, or slabs, weighing about seven hundred and fifty pounds each, and shipped the slabs by truck to the refinery to separate the gold and silver from the copper. This was the long and grueling process that workers went through in order to make copper wire and other products.

The copper industry suffered a downturn due to changing technologies, and has only recently emerged into a renaissance. But during the first three decades of the twentieth century it played a major role in Arizona's economy, and my father and his co-workers labored mightily and at very low pay.[13]

My father possessed several noteworthy personal qualities that left a deep impression on me. He maintained a sincere interest in people and their efforts to improve their lives. He had a natural ability to lead others, and wherever he worked he emerged as a leader of some cause or another. Further, he always expressed interest in political life, and I sensed he had a great deal of political acumen. He subscribed to two Spanish language newspapers, one from Los Angeles, *El Diario La Prensa,* and the other from San Antonio, Texas, *La Prensa.* He made me sit beside him while he read aloud the political news and the editorial pages about the labor movement and revolutions in Mexico. Although I wanted to go outside and play with my friends, he made me sit there and listen. I never understood why I was the only one of his children who experienced this type of parental attention.[14]

From left, formal portraits of my father, Francisco, circa 1928, and me, circa 1940. *Photo courtesy of author.*

In Pirtleville my father organized the community festivities for Cinco de Mayo and for El Diez y Seis de Septiembre (September 16), Mexican Independence Day. The adults constructed a wooden platform and floor so people could dance. In addition, local leaders made speeches, and vendors sold hot dogs, enchiladas, tacos, and drinks. My father, whom everyone called Don Francisco or Don Pancho, terms of respect, always delivered one of the speeches. He took part in the annual tug-of-war on the Fourth of July between the Calumet and Arizona Smelter workers in Douglas, where he worked, and the miners in Bisbee. Six people lined up on each side, and they pulled on a chain with a flag in the middle. On the other side there were usually big, strong, heavyset Yugoslavian miners from Bisbee, but my father was big, and he was always the headman for the Douglas smelter. They usually won because of his strength. It was a great rivalry, and the contests played a noteworthy part in building a sense of border community and culture.[15]

Ten children required that both my parents worked, so my mother became a midwife. She had served as an assistant to a midwife in Cananea, and she utilized that practical experience to find her economic niche. Ultimately she took some medical courses in Arizona and secured her Arizona midwife's license. Her reputation in Cochise County grew, and whenever a new baby entered the world my mother answered the call. She delivered most of the children in Pirtleville, and years later, after we moved to Douglas, she delivered many Mexican babies in the community.[16] On several occasions I assisted with her deliveries, and later this experience bore direct benefits when I owned a horse farm on River Road and Dodge in Tucson. When the animals were in foal, my job was to oversee the foaling process, and sometimes, during a particularly difficult birth, I rolled up my sleeves, pulled the legs on the colt, and managed to complete the job.[17]

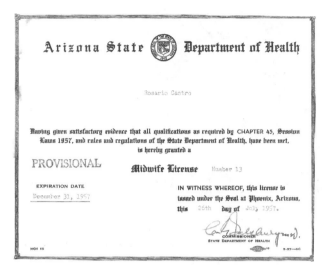

My mother's provisional midwife's license, 1957. *Photo courtesy of author.*

My mother also became a curandera, a person who treated people suffering from ailments. She developed expertise in herbs, potions, and medicinal plants. Everyone had great faith in her ability, and when anyone got sick, they called upon "Chalita," a term of endearment and nickname by which she was widely known in Cochise County. She became skilled in treating malaria, stomach problems, fever, and all kinds of other ailments and illnesses. She had her own home recipes, herbs, and teas, and her patients depended on her. She usually accepted a fifty-pound can of lard, a hundred-pound sack of beans, or a chicken or two as payment for services. This form of barter system actually served her well because with so many children to feed, particularly after my father's death, she needed food. After my father's passing, for example, she sent me out into the desert to collect saguaro fruit, prickly pear fruit, and mesquite beans. I brought these fruits and vegetables home so she could prepare them to eat. She expressed great pleasure in never seeking welfare from the state or from the community at large.[18]

My mother, like my father, was not overly affectionate with us children. She never kissed or hugged us when we went to bed at night. I know she loved us dearly, but she had her hands full with all of us. In order to survive and feed us, she ran our house like a marine boot camp, and everyone had to contribute to the household. Although she was diminutive in stature, she commanded respect. One of the outcomes of this lack of affection, perhaps, was my difficulty as an adult in showing affection outwardly, even to those closest to me.

My mother was also very much a part of the Mexican culture. When my father died, for example, she went into mourning for twenty-five years, wearing black for that entire time. She also had my sister, Enriqueta, wear

My mother (date unknown).
*Photo courtesy of author.*

black. My sister wore black for the first year or two of high school, and, noticing that the students ridiculed her, I told my mother that we lived in the United States, and my sister must have a life. My mother, fortunately, relented on this cultural issue.

Indeed, public education in the 1920s and 1930s served as a kind of social and cultural crucible for me. Between forty and fifty children crammed the classrooms in the Mexican schools. Few books or instructional materials were available. Teachers were young and inexperienced, and we always spoke Spanish on the playground. In the classroom, of course, we spoke English, which, to most of us, was a foreign language. My hands turned black and blue on several occasions as the teacher rapped my knuckles for speaking Spanish. In an environment not geared to optimum educational outcomes, most Mexican children remained in school for very short periods. My older brothers illustrated this point as they quit the public education system prior to entering high school. Like so many others of their ilk, they sought work in the mines or smelter, thus sealing their professional fates.

Somehow I survived grammar school, and when I went to middle school it was the first time I shared a classroom with Anglo children. The schools had adopted a tracking system, so students were divided into four groups—A1, A2, A3, and A4. A1 classes were for the top students, and A4 classes were for the least able. Predictably, as Mexican children were supposedly deficient in English, administrators placed us in an A4 class. Knowing the caste system, I was determined to move up and out as quickly as possible, and soon was moved to an A1 class. On one occasion in the sixth grade the bell rang for recess, and as I ran out of the classroom to the playground, I overheard two teachers in conversation. One asked the other how she liked her assignment that year, and the other replied, "I hate it. I've got one of the A4 classes with all of those dumb Mexican kids." I decided then that I would not be a "dumb Mexican kid," and that some day in the future I would have her job. From that day forward I always completed homework assignments, sometimes staying up until two or three in the morning. Often my mother advised me that it was late, and I should go to bed and then get up early to finish my assignments.

Something else altered my attitudes. My sixth grade teacher, Eileen Wright, approached my desk, placed her hand on my shoulder, and said, "Raúl, you have a lot of potential, but you're lazy. You're not doing the job." The fact that she touched my shoulder and spoke to me in that manner made me think, *Whoa, this teacher must like me. She's interested in me and she wants me to do things.* The next day I arrived with a new attitude, prepared to become a better student. Many years later when I was sworn in as governor of Arizona, a telegram from Seattle, Washington, arrived at the governor's office with the question, "Are you the same Raúl Castro I had in the sixth grade in Douglas, Arizona? Signed Eileen Wright." I called her and said that I was. She expressed her amazement and pride, and this was a particularly emotional moment for me as I reflected on my education and youth.[19]

During my middle school years, a particularly disturbing cultural practice existed at the school. At recess students played a game called "race against race." On one side were the Anglos, and on the other side were the Mexicans. We lined up facing each other then slugged and threw rocks at the other side. Dirt and blood filled the playground, and I was always perplexed that the school did nothing to curtail the odious practice. Douglas in the 1920s was, underneath it all, a community divided.

High school proved another matter. Everyone attended the only high school in town, Douglas High School. And, unlike middle school, it seemed like a family. I counted among my friends Anglo students as well as Mexican students. Whether everyone had matured or the larger society was slowly changing, Douglas High School encouraged a social environment that lowered barriers, diminished mistrust and prejudice, and brought a degree of harmony to those of us who lived on the border. These years of enlightenment may have indirectly led me into foreign diplomacy as one of my professions.

Some of the lighter and more entertaining aspects of my formative years on the Arizona-Sonora border reflected the community's cultural diversity and sense of regional identity. Two local merchants, José Robles and Gertrudis Estrada, owned a store and, in an inspired move prompted by their contacts with the larger and worldly business community in Tucson, they acquired the first radio in Pirtleville. This RCA radio, with the distinctive logo of a dog with ears attuned toward the large horn, prompted a community-wide get-together. The intrepid local entrepreneurs sent out invitations for everyone to come to a dance, the music to be supplied by this new technological innovation. For the occasion they rented a two-story building with a dance floor. No one in Pirtleville had any idea what a radio was, so everyone rushed to the big event. As it turned out, storms swept into southern Arizona and northern Sonora that evening, and static, rather than music, filled the airwaves. Nevertheless, I attended the first public radio event in Pirtleville.

Another more significant occasion centered on George W. P. Hunt, Arizona's first governor after statehood, and his visit to Douglas. The media referred to him as "the Old Walrus." His obese five foot nine frame was punctuated with thick glasses and a huge walrus moustache. Hunt, re-elected governor of Arizona seven different times between 1912 and 1930, dominated Arizona politics for nearly two decades, and his Progressive reforms and intractable nature formed his enduring legacy. He attended a Fourth of July celebration in one of his numerous quests for re-election. The day was sultry, and he was dressed in his usual white linen suit. I hurried over to the park because organizers provided free hot dogs, hamburgers, and sodas, while the adults could consume free beer. After all had had their fill, Hunt delivered his speech up on the bandstand platform in the Tenth Street Park. At one point he looked over at us, pointed right at me, and said, "In this great state of ours, anyone can be governor. Why even one of those little barefooted Mexican kids sitting over there could one day be governor."[20] That same bandstand platform where Hunt delivered his political speech and pointed at me remains at that park on Tenth Street. In 2002, city leaders renamed it The Raúl H. Castro Park. I considered that recognition a distinct honor, but the hypocrisy on the corner across from that park remained. The Elks Lodge, the same Elks Lodge that I could never join because they prohibited Mexicans from membership, reminded me of the other, less tolerant side of my formative years.[21]

# CHAPTER II

## HIGH SCHOOL AND THE WORLD BEYOND

In 1931 I entered Douglas High School and spent four transformative years there. Naturally the Great Depression provided the economic and cultural context between my freshman year and my graduation in 1935. The dour economic climate shaped and influenced all of our lives on the border. I read the *Douglas Daily Dispatch, El Diario de Agua Prieta,* and Tucson's *Arizona Daily Star* each day and discerned that not only had the Arizona-Sonora border been affected by the economic collapse, but also Tucson, Hermosillo, Los Angeles, and New York—indeed the entire world—experienced unprecedented shocks to their economies, cultures, and political lives. Everyone I knew was poor, but that made little difference to me; we were always poor. The stock market crash of 1929 made little difference in our daily lives.[1]

I found a job at S. H. Kress & Company in Douglas cleaning the windows, stocking shelves, and sweeping up around the store. The job generated a small amount of spending money, though I always gave a portion of my wages to my mother. At home, eleven of us, including my mother, squeezed into a small three-bedroom house. All of my older brothers dropped out of school early, and some left after only one year. Others went further, but none entered high school, and all went to work in the smelter. My sister attended high school for two years, but only my younger brother, Ernesto, and I graduated from high school.[2]

Perhaps Ernesto and I, as the two youngest siblings, had an advantage. I heard my older brothers heading to work early in the morning, long before I left for high school, and dragging themselves home at three-thirty or four in the afternoon. They were sweaty, dirty, and very tired. Worse, the smelter had segregated showers with signs that read "Americans Only" and "Mexicans Only." The Mexican showers were inadequate, if they functioned at all, and, as a practical matter, Mexican workers were unable to shower after work. So my brothers, filthy and covered with dust, escaped into an alcohol haze on a nightly basis. At night three or four of us shared the same bed, and the stench from the liquor disrupted my sleep and taught me some valuable lessons.[3]

I thought, *Do I want to be like my brothers? Will I be working the rest of my life in the smelter or the mines like them? Is this all there is?* It bothered me. *No, I don't want that!* I wanted to be like the banker, Mr. Crowell, manager of the Bank of Douglas, whom I saw walking to work in his black suit, or like Mr. Otis, in his suit and tie, opening the J. C. Penney store, and I would ask myself, *What do I have to do to be like them?*

I noted that Mexicans comprised the vast majority of the physical labor workforce in Douglas, and indeed in all of the communities on the American side of the border. Few held professional positions. There were no Mexicans working in any government jobs or in any stores or offices. Moreover, I learned early in my teenage years that Phelps Dodge held no jobs in their offices for someone like me. The symbolism of the time taught me that my destiny was that of a laborer. Like my older brothers, the smelter beckoned me, and even if I worked there my salary would be less than Anglo workers. I decided that education held the key to breaking away from the undesirable, debilitating fate that had engulfed my older brothers.[4]

Like most of my high school classmates, I walked to school each day, and my route took me past Tenth Street and D Avenue. One day I noticed an elderly Anglo man with his dog, sitting on the sidewalk in front of the house. He wore khaki pants, an old gray jacket, and chewed tobacco. He greeted me and struck up a pleasant conversation. Soon we chatted on a regular basis, and he always wanted to converse in Spanish. He seemed cordial, friendly, and down-to-earth, and I enjoyed teaching him new words and phrases in Spanish. Later I learned that the kindly man was an Arizona legend, "Rawhide Jimmy" Douglas.[5]

Rawhide Jimmy was the son of Dr. James Douglas, who discovered the Copper Queen Mine north of Douglas, near Bisbee. He played a major role in making Phelps Dodge Corporation a giant, and Douglas, Arizona, was named for him.[6] Rawhide Jimmy grew to be as famous as his father. In 1912 he moved to Jerome, Arizona, in the copper-rich north central part of the new state of Arizona. He purchased the Little Daisy Mine, also known as the United Verde Extension Mine. After four years and sinking a half million dollars into the enterprise, he hit a vein of pure copper five feet wide. In 1916 the mines produced ten million dollars in gold, silver, and copper. As a teenager who conversed in Spanish with him on my way to school, I knew nothing of his remarkable past. To me he seemed a kindly old man, dressed in rugged common clothes, who liked to speak Spanish.[7]

His son, Lewis Douglas, who was born in Bisbee, Arizona, graduated from Amherst College and was attending MIT graduate school when he was commissioned as second lieutenant in World War I. After the war he worked briefly for his father at the Little Daisy Mine in Jerome but soon left to teach history at Amherst. He quickly returned to Arizona and entered politics. He was elected to the Arizona House of Representatives in 1922 and served until 1926, when he ran for the United States House of Representatives seat vacated by Carl Hayden, who had been promoted by the people of Arizona to a seat in the US Senate.[8]

Congressman Douglas served three terms, and on March 7, 1933, President Franklin Delano Roosevelt appointed him director of the budget. Eighteen months later he resigned after breaking with the Roosevelt administration and denouncing deficit spending. From 1947 to 1951 he served as ambassador to Great Britain. In his long and distinguished career in business and in politics, Lewis Douglas projected himself in a very different way compared to his father, Rawhide Jimmy. Lewis always wore a black suit, coat and tie, a patch on his eye, and arrived at events in a big black limousine. He was aloof and had little in common to those of us who had grown up along the border. In the early 1950s, shortly after his stint as ambassador to Great Britain, he moved into offices in downtown Tucson, and I began a series of weekly lunches with him. He enjoyed reminiscing about politics, diplomacy, and Arizona history. I found it unusual that Ambassador Douglas usually wanted to talk all afternoon, but I had to get back to work.[9] Moreover, we had little in common; I maintained a more deeply held connection with his father, Rawhide Jimmy.[10] I knew the Douglas family quite well and respected their inextricable ties with Arizona's economic and political history.

School and its possibilities separated me from my world at home. I was determined to excel in the classroom and interscholastic sports. Success in either realm, I reasoned, could distinguish me from my contemporaries and provide me with options otherwise not available.

Sports played a major role in developing my self-confidence and exposed me to the spirit of teamwork. I quarterbacked for the high school football team. I also played basketball in spite of the fact that my height limited my effectiveness. Our basketball coach, Milton Morse, served as a role model, and I admired his ability to instill discipline into our approach to the game. My best sport was track, where I ran the half-mile and the mile relay. Sports helped me form friendships, learn valuable lessons, and grow in ways I had not thought possible.

Playing first-string quarterback for the Douglas High School football team proved a highlight in my early life. All the players enjoyed one another, and we had fun. I worked mightily for the starting position and winning the competition made me feel successful. I craved the attention, status, and peer approval that came with the quarterback position.

Still, prejudice and intolerance found their way, somewhat indirectly, into high school football. Many of the players joined a group called Junior Hi-Y, which met at the local YMCA on Tenth Street.[11] Though the meetings ended in the early evening, it was often very hot, and the players all wanted to go swimming in the YMCA pool. Everyone poured into the pool area. I arrived last, and as I was about to enter the door closed on me and the YMCA director said, "Raúl Castro, you can't go in there."

"Why not?" I replied.

"Because Mexican kids can only swim on Saturday afternoon," he shot back.

The pool was dirtiest on Saturday afternoon, and that was when the maintenance people conducted the weekly cleaning of the pool. So I went home while all of my friends went swimming. But as I slowly walked out, feeling like dirt, I looked up on the wall of the building and read the sign "Young Men's Christian Association," and thought, *I don't see anything Christian about that.* I decided then that I would change the rule some day, and later, when I worked as Pima County deputy attorney in Tucson, I was selected to serve on the board of directors of the YMCA. I immediately, convinced the board to change the discriminatory rule.[12]

Athletics and organized sports, notwithstanding occasional bouts with racial prejudice, brought me closer to my classmates and teachers. The latter group, however, suggested that balance among athletics, academics, and social development was desirable, if not necessary, for growth and success. C. E. "Pop" Wilson, my English teacher, took an interest in me and helped to broaden my world view. One day he approached me and said, "Raúl, why don't you take journalism?"

My immature response: "Mr. Wilson, I'm a football player. Journalism doesn't quite fit with a football player."

"You can't play football all of your life," he retorted.

The exchange convinced me to take journalism, and as a result I became the editor of our school newspaper, the *Border Bulldog*, and it provided me with tremendous insight for my adult years, because later in life I worked in journalism and I dealt with the written and electronic media when I campaigned for elective office.[13]

Shortly thereafter he asked, "Raúl, why don't you take drama?"

I growled in response, "Mr. Wilson, drama? I'm a football player. It's not in my line."

But I respected him, discerned he cared about me, and therefore I considered this second improbable proposition. So I debuted as the male lead in *Old Lady 31*, thinking to myself, *Whoever heard of a Mexican kid acting in the male lead part in a high school-produced play in Douglas, Arizona?* But Pop Wilson exposed me to this cultural form, and I benefited from it.[14]

I played an old man in a nursing home with thirty-one women who one day disappeared and got drunk. My character returned to the nursing home at two A.M., still intoxicated, and was supposed to collapse gently onto the horsehair couch on stage. Instead, I jumped onto the sofa like a football player and caused the leg to break off, which in turn catapulted me offstage, into the music pit, and onto the piano. The audience roared with laughter because they thought it was part of the play. My career as an actor was short-lived, but I appreciated Pop Wilson's interest in me, and I enjoyed this brief experience in the performing arts.

My response to the attention from teachers Eileen Wright and Pop Wilson revealed something more. I enjoyed standing out and was not content to remain a member of a group. My ambition served as a vehicle for recognition. This trait stemmed in part from the fact that I was raised in a family of ten children where there was little personal attention, and I always looked for someone to care about me. Eileen Wright and Pop Wilson both cared, and their acts of humanity in that regard influenced me in profound ways and made me realize that grammar school and high school teachers shape lives.

In recent years people have asked me about the "back to basics" movement, cutting out sports, music, and art in our public schools. Those activities have always paid huge dividends for our society. They tap the well of potential and encourage students to work with groups, a necessary skill set to function in the economy. Sports, music, drama, and journalism added greatly to my high school experience as well as to my growth, development, and maturation. I concluded early in life that participation in school activities led to a sense of citizenship and community involvement. Furthermore, extra-curricular activities instilled in me the concept of volunteerism; I gave of myself to contribute to my school and was part of something bigger than myself. Later, as I peered down at young offenders in my role as a juvenile court judge, I realized again that extra-curricular activities were sometimes the only things that kept children in school. I knew also that without those options I could have ended up lost and working in the smelter.[15]

As I approached high school graduation, the principal asked, "Raúl, what are your plans?" I replied that I wanted to go to college. Incredibly, he took me into his office and told me, "You know we are living in a border community, and it is almost impossible to get Mexican children opportunities or jobs here. I would recommend that you don't go to college because you will be wasting your time and money. I will give you a letter saying that you are totally bilingual, and that you would be a tremendous asset to a business in the community." He drafted the letter and gave it to me.[16] He then sent me over to the superintendent of schools who mimicked the message about our border community and the lack of opportunity. He added that I was a fine student, but dreams for professional or economic advancement, especially for a young Mexican man, were not possible, and college would be a waste of my time, energy, and money. I rejected their culturally-biased advice.

Fortunately, at the same time the high school administrators were informing me that I was destined for a life of poverty on the border I received an athletic scholarship from Arizona State Teachers College in Flagstaff, now Northern Arizona University. As I stepped on the ladder to clean a window at work, somebody tapped me on the shoulder. I turned, and a man introduced himself and said that he taught industrial arts at Arizona State Teachers College. He mentioned that he had learned that I was a pretty good quarterback, and he wanted to give me a football scholarship to play for the Lumberjacks. I was stunned. Words poured forth as I said I had grown interested in teaching, and I wanted make some kind of difference in the world. I told him that I worked my way into National Honor Society and had graduated in the upper level of my class. In addition to sports and getting good grades, I continued, I became involved in journalism and acting. The recruiter smiled and said quietly that he knew all of this about me. We shook hands, and I ran home. When I told my mother about the visitor and the scholarship, she beamed with pride and told me to jump at this opportunity. So in the fall of 1935, as the global depression lingered on with no end in sight, I left for Flagstaff, Arizona, focused on changing my life and improving the lives of others.[17]

# CHAPTER III

## CRUCIBLE OF OPTIMISM:
## HIGHER EDUCATION AT ARIZONA STATE
## TEACHERS COLLEGE IN FLAGSTAFF

On September 1, 1935, a blast of cold wind greeted me as I disembarked from the bus in downtown Flagstaff, Arizona, and gazed upon the inspiring geologic gift of the San Francisco Peaks, which towered above the small city of eighteen thousand people. Flagstaff, located on a much traveled and historic crossroads, sits at a breathtaking seventy-two hundred feet above sea level. Historically the area served as a rest stop for Indians, Spaniards, Mexicans, and, after the American takeover of this region in 1848, an increasing number of Anglo travelers. Between 1857 and 1860, an impossibly divided US Congress, wrestling with the thorny political problems associated with organizing the western territories, sent Lieutenant Edward F. Beale to survey the recently acquired lands and create a road across what would become northern Arizona. Beale sent glowing reports to Congress, advising that this portion of the vast territory, what was then northern New Mexico, was rich in grasslands, water, and timber. Once established, the Beale Road became a well-traveled thoroughfare for emigrants to California. One party of sojourners from Boston, planning to settle in the Little Colorado River area thirty miles east of Winslow, camped at a small spring with the San Francisco Peaks looming overhead. On July 4, 1876, in honor of the nation's centennial, they stripped a nearby pine tree of its branches and bark and raised an American flag. When the party moved on to their destination, their "flagstaff" remained for those who followed and provided the remote northern Arizona town with a distinct name of patriotic origins.[1]

Curious and excited, I entered an academic environment forged on the American southwestern frontier of timber, saw mills, and railroads. Originally called Northern Arizona Normal School, my college was only thirty-six years old and was formed on September 1, 1899. Just eleven years prior to my matriculation, the State of Arizona recognized the school and allowed it to award the Bachelor of Education degree. With this institutional academic promotion, the school renamed itself Northern Arizona State Teacher's College, and in 1929 the name was changed again to Arizona State Teacher's College in Flagstaff (ASTC), the school that accepted me as a freshman in 1935.[2] Former ASTC president Grady Gammage, who served there from 1926-1933 and then moved to Tempe for the next twenty-eight years to transform what was Arizona State Teacher's College at Tempe into Arizona State University, called our education in Flagstaff in the 1930s a "Depression Industry"; one that fared well in hard times.

The Depression shaped my college experience, though its impact on my four years in Flagstaff differed in marked ways from my high school experience in Douglas. I recall "prune pickers" from California, farm children, and other sons and daughters from mining families like mine, but we were a homogonous student body. Financial aid and an acceptance of ethnic and cultural diversity were somewhat foreign to me, but I welcomed these tastes of the world beyond the border. Besides a greater degree of ethnic tolerance, our little college community was a model of togetherness and respect in this rather isolated portion of the Southwest. One of my friends, Ida Mae Fredericks Nowabbi Murdock,[3] was a Hopi from First Mesa and always told me that she was accepted and experienced no discrimination in her years at school in Flagstaff. In fact, she was the first Hopi Indian to obtain a degree from ASTC when she graduated with me in 1939. Furthermore, we could boast of sustainability at ASTC because we produced our own electricity with a steam-powered generator, and student bakers and cooks provided breads, cakes, pies and other foodstuffs in our state-of-the-art kitchen and commissary for the entire student body.

One of my good friends, Jeff Ferris, later noted that "the student body was all in the same economic group. We were all poor, but we didn't know it," he said, and I agreed with his assessment. Few of my fellow ASTC Lumberjacks could rely on their families for financial support during their college years. Most had to work for room, board, and tuition, just like me. In-state tuition and fees ranged from $225 per year in 1935 to $279 in 1939 when I graduated. Some students were creative in paying for their education: Elsie McCauley bartered sacks of potatoes for tuition, and Rolf Larson's Holstein cow, Codera, underwrote his education at ASTC in the 1930s.

The part-time work program of the New Deal's National Youth Administration (NYA) helped several of my friends mitigate the cost of college. In 1939, for example, NYA awarded ASTC $5,940, which supported 443 students, and seniors were often asked to give up their NYA jobs so that the freshman could work. The dairy and the dining hall, where I eventually worked, were two areas on campus that benefitted from the New Deal's NYA program.[4]

My football scholarship turned out to be far from glamorous, and it became a lesson in campus sustainability. I had a job washing dishes three times a day in the cafeteria's kitchen. I worked up the proverbial food chain, and soon I was promoted to assistant cook. I received compliments on my meatloaf with tomato purée but eventually left the kitchen for the "front of the house" and waited tables. In that job I wore a little white coat and tie and was assigned to wait on the table of university president, Dr. Thomas Tormey.[5] I reported to "Mother" Margaret Hanley, whose name was synonymous with the dining hall, and under her watchful eye I learned a great deal about manners and etiquette of the day, all of which served me well in later years.

In order to attend school, I cobbled together several sources of funds. Much like students today, I forged a host of creative mechanisms in order to make ends meet and achieve good grades. In addition to my scholarship I enlisted in the army national guard, which provided twenty-five dollars per month and generated enough money to pay for tuition, books, meals, and my dormitory room. I was stationed in Flagstaff and commissioned to the I Company. We drilled once a week and trained at Fort Huachuca during the summer, which in those days still had Apache Indian scouts and continued to practice a segregated military as white officers oversaw African American enlisted troops.[6] When I first joined the national guard the authorities refused to accept me because I was still a Mexican citizen. I immediately applied for American citizenship and was readmitted to the guard for the four years I attended ASTC.[7]

I returned home in the summers of 1936 and 1937 and lived in the same small house with my mother and siblings. While I was there I raised additional funds by working at the smelter. In that first summer of my freshman year a young man named Stewart Carpenter, a foreman for Phelps Dodge, looked at me and said, "Castro, I want you to get a crew of ten men and pick up that I-beam and put it over there." It was a very heavy, long I-beam that could not possibly be lifted by ten men without everyone suffering a hernia. I told him that the smelter had a bull gang for doing such jobs, and they also had all kinds of equipment for picking up heavy material without anyone getting hurt. He replied, "That's the trouble with you goddamn Mexican kids. You go to school and you already think you own the world. You're fired. Get out of here."[8]

As I left the smelter, the superintendent, John McDaniels, stopped me and asked where I was going at that time of day. I told him that Carpenter had fired me. Mr. McDaniels said, "Forget about Carpenter, you aren't fired, and please head down to work in the converters." Mr. McDaniels knew me from high school since I was good friends with his son and daughter and had been over to his home on numerous occasions. In this instance it was who I knew rather than what I knew, but a different Mexican worker would not have been saved in this manner, and I filed away this lesson for future reference.

In the summer of 1937 I decided that the smelter workers needed a union. None before had existed. I told the workers that there should be no wage difference and separate showers were discriminatory. As my father had in the teens and twenties, I gave speeches and excited many of my co-workers. Unlike my father, however, I possessed no labor organizing skills. And I seemed to forget that I was returning to Flagstaff to continue my college education. So I contacted Orville Larson, a professional union organizer from Jerome, and persuaded him to come down to Douglas. My brother Nacho, Castulo Sanchez, and I formed the union movement and rented a makeshift union hall at the corner of Eighth Street and G Avenue on the second floor, above a restaurant. Larson moved to Douglas, organized the workforce at the smelter, and succeeded in establishing the first labor union in the smelter: the Mine Mill Smelter Workers of America. I returned to college while Castulo and Nacho negotiated with Phelps Dodge and obtained the first union contract in 1937.[9]

Years later, when I was practicing law in Tucson in the early 1950s, the union asked if I would represent them. I refused for several reasons including the fact that its headquarters had moved to Denver and the leadership there had moved too far to the political left for my comfort. At that time another union, the Steel Workers of America, had formed in the smelter, and by 1950 there were two unions representing the workers there. But the one started when I was in college remained, and it represented one of my first acts of organizational politics in my developing career.

As my summer activities reflected, public engagement and social activism began to percolate to the surface of my consciousness while sports took on a different kind of psychological meaning in my college experience. At ASTC I played football for only two years. The college had a freshman team and a varsity team. The first year I was quarterback on the freshman team. My sophomore year I played for the varsity but weighed only 140 pounds. I lacked size, so I looked around for an alternative athletic activity. I made good grades and ran track, but my need for attention was not fulfilled in football. That need could be filled, I reasoned, by joining the collegiate boxing team. I was willing to take the chance that I might lose, but I wanted the chance to win, so I left football and became a boxer.

Boxing was simple and direct; my job was to get into the ring with my opponent and destroy him. By succeeding in this regard, I thought I could achieve the individual recognition I craved. People would know me on campus and say, "Hi Raúl, you are a great guy," and that is exactly what happened. I became an accomplished boxer and still have a commemorative plaque that reads:

Raúl H. Castro, Boxing, Football, Track 1935-1939.
Member, Northern Arizona University Hall of Fame.
Sponsored by Valley National Bank.

Raúl Castro's greatest athletic accomplishment while attending Arizona State Teacher's College was as a member of the boxing team, fighting as a welter weight in the competitive Border Conference.[10] Castro went undefeated as a collegiate boxer, as the all Border Conference boxing champion. He was the Arizona State welterweight champion in 1938 and was elected captain of the team by his teammates. Also in 1938 Castro was the Border Conference half-mile track champion and team captain. Raúl H. Castro later served the State of Arizona as the Pima County attorney, superior court judge and governor. On behalf of the United States he served as ambassador to El Salvador, Bolivia, and Argentina.

I joined a number of collegiate clubs, which further entrenched me into collegiate culture and filled other needs for recognition. I was a part of the Newman Club, the A Club, the International Relations Club, the Spanish Club, Phi Sigma Iota, Kappa Delta Pi, and I served as ASTC Senior Class Treasurer. Still, the highlight of my college days encompassed boxing, track and academic achievement.

I devoted countless hours to study and worked hard at my college course work. I wanted to make the best grades because that was the way to social and professional advancement and upward mobility. My induction into the National Honor Society in high school made me proud, but President Tormey raised this sense of accomplishment to a new level when, one day while I served him lunch, he said, "Raúl, take your jacket off. I want you to come over and sit with us. You are having lunch with us." He told me that I had just been admitted into Phi Kappa Phi, a national scholastic honor fraternity, and added that my days of waiting tables were over. I became a member of the honor fraternity and grew to know the president of the college, both of which aided my quest for upward mobility and recognition.

I sought a teaching degree, with a major in education and a minor in business. I had to take courses in several different areas, including art and music. I had little confidence in either area, so I braced myself for an uphill climb. I had an art instructor, Miss Case, who delivered an unlikely dissertation on how she had found that Mexican children were unusually artistic and very musical. She was predisposed that I would do well in her course. She had no idea that I was color blind, and my efforts fell far below her expectations. So I was farmed out to help another art teacher, Miss Pachinka, who went to all of the public schools in Flagstaff. I became her escort and would carry her crayons and pass them out along with the paper in her public school classes. I helped with the students, and that is how I received the art credit for my teaching degree. That challenge took some creativity, but I still had to complete the music credit. The course, Music and Harmony Theory, required that I compose an original song and play it on the piano. I was tone deaf, but somehow I persevered and finished the course and received my music credit.

While I survived art and music, I embraced with alacrity my course of practice teaching. I taught sixth grade at the Beaver School, near the college campus. My supervising instructor was Bob Robles, a wonderful teacher and an inspiration to me. Beaver School in 1938-1939 remained segregated, and I taught Navajo, Hopi, Mexican, and Spanish-Basque children.[11] I thoroughly enjoyed my practice teaching experience, and the semester at Beaver School left a profound imprint on me. In fact, later in life I have been asked which occupation I liked the best, and without question it was teaching. I found it rewarding and crucial to the future of our democratic society. Of course, the profession was a lot less stressful in the 1930s and 1940s, but classroom teaching and its rewards have never left me.

My graduating class counted seventy-four baccalaureates. Yet a remarkable number of them found hope in desperate economic times and appreciated the chance to get a college education. Their level of pride in accomplishment was high as a result of the financial struggle. This pride, combined with a cooperative atmosphere at the school, especially during my last two years on campus—epitomized by friendship, respect, and closeness—made these four years a kind of crucible of optimism. In fact, during my last year in college, campus conditions began to improve. The total budget was $213,635 compared to a low of $158,324 in 1934 and

1935. Steam heat replaced coal furnaces in the dormitories by the end of my tenure there, and the Business Department found enough money in its budget to purchase a Dictaphone. In the fall of 1939 enrollment swelled to 545 students.[12]

In June of 1939, I graduated with a Bachelor of Arts degree. I was a teacher. I had good academic credentials, graduating in the top 10 percent of my class. I was a good athlete and I planned to return to Douglas, Arizona, to teach school and live the good life. I had left depression-ridden Douglas in 1935 and hoped to return there to make it better. After four years of broadening my horizons, performing on a bigger stage, experiencing people from other cultures, learning new forms of discipline and sacrifice, and honing a new set of professional skills, I looked forward to the next chapter in my life. In the spring of 1939, like so many of my fellow college graduates, I thought I had completed my college education but was entirely unaware that another kind of education, grassroots in nature, was about to begin.

# CHAPTER IV

## RETURN TO THE BORDERLANDS

Gerald D. Nash, the preeminent economic historian of the modern West, argued that the region "changed masters" during the Depression, substituting the federal government for its colonial dependence on eastern capital. Yet Arizona relied on large federal spending since the territorial period (1863-1912), when the army provided security for Arizona citizens and markets for Arizona produce and livestock.[1] For example, the Newlands Reclamation Act of 1902 provided for federally subsidized irrigation, including the Roosevelt Dam and the Salt River Project. And the military's demand for fiber brought on the cotton boom of World War I, which impacted Pima and Pinal County agriculturalists profoundly. The New Deal in Arizona, therefore, was not a radical break with precedent, but instead deepened and broadened Arizona's dependence on federal funding and influence. By the end of the 1930s federal officials in various agencies were subsidizing agriculture; supervising enormous irrigation projects; regulating grazing and forest harvesting; and dispersing grants, loans, and relief to individuals, businesses, and municipalities. The federal government, incredibly, spent three times the per capita national average in Western states, including Arizona. Much of the federal largesse poured into Arizona's extractive industries, like copper. Yet federal investment in recreational facilities, highway construction, education, and municipal government, combined with an expanded transportation network, enabled the remarkable urbanization of Arizona during World War II and the postwar era.

In 1940 few of my fellow Arizona citizens could have imagined the changes about to take place. The state's manufacturing industry was in its infancy, and Phoenix, Arizona's largest city, counted only 65,414 in population. In 1934 a Phoenix-based advertising firm created the phrase "Valley of the Sun" to replace "Salt River Valley" and to promote tourism in Phoenix and central Arizona. It quickly came to symbolize the dreams of a new and emerging business elite, like Barry Goldwater, Frank Snell, and Walter Bimson, all of whom I worked with during my legal and political career in

Arizona. Though the thirty-five thousand visitors to the Phoenix area in 1939-1940 stayed at or toured the Arizona Biltmore and other new resorts and attractions, the center of power—both political and economic—remained at the venerated Adams Hotel in downtown Phoenix where farmers, mining executives, and cattlemen purchased legislators' votes and ran the state. Arizona's political culture at the time—a mix of eastern colonialism, western individualism, and southern Jim Crowism—remained rooted in the extractive economy. I viewed establishment power and politics in Arizona from afar, never imagining that twenty-five years later I would be at the center of it all.[2]

In the summer of 1939 I was twenty-three years old, a college graduate, and I decided to return to Douglas to become an American citizen and apply for teaching jobs. I remember the citizenship ceremony well, and that day, November 21, 1939, remains one of the most important in my life. I was sworn in as an American citizen in the superior court in Bisbee, the Cochise County seat. Securing a teaching position proved more challenging. The school board, administrators told me, maintained a policy of not hiring Mexican American teachers. A Mexican American teacher had been on the district payroll there for many years, they added, but the board had decided, as a matter of policy, not to hire any more Mexican American teachers. I was an American citizen, but it made no difference. Undaunted, I looked for a teaching job. I applied in Pomerene, Arizona, a small rural community just north of Benson. I interviewed with a member of the school board, and rather than discussing teaching methods or curriculum, he asked if I could ride a horse and rope a steer. I replied that I had applied for a teaching position, not to be a cowboy on a ranching operation. Not surprisingly, the school board turned down my application. I then applied for a teaching slot in Ajo, the copper community in western Pima County. In 1939 the community was segregated, and the Mexican miners lived separate and unequal lives from the Anglo managers of the mine and smelter. That application process proved futile as well, and the position was ultimately awarded to an Anglo American. It seemed that the various school boards in southern Arizona should have advised that "Mexican Americans need not apply."

Realizing the increasing role that the federal government played in all aspects of life in Arizona, I decided to apply for a job as a mail carrier. I also applied at the Federal Bureau of Investigation and other federal postings. I took the civil service examination, passed with high scores, but not once did an agency call me for an interview. I decided to leave Douglas and informed my family that I was unable to find a teaching position or any other entry-level professional job. My mother called a family meeting and said, "Raúl is leaving us because he can't get a job here."

My brother Alfonso reacted quickly, "Let's go back to Mexico."

And then Ernesto, disgusted, chimed in, "Yeah, let's go back to Mexico."

My mother cried out, "We are not going back to Mexico! We have a responsibility to this government. It has been good to us. You've been educated and you all have a job. What else do you want? Raúl must leave. But any of the rest of you who leave this house and return to Mexico without fulfilling your obligation to this government is no son of mine, and there is the door. You can come back here whenever you want, but there is the door."[3] The cathartic moment ended in silence, and no one left the United States. Alfonso, the brother who said, "Let's go back to Mexico," later retired as a colonel from the US Army.[4]

After saying our goodbyes, and with the prayers of my mother, I headed for the Douglas train station. I caught the first freight train for El Paso. I was on the road and lived like a hobo. I rode the freights all over the country for a year or two, boxing when I could, and working in the fields whenever possible. I remained a skilled boxer, and made fifty, one hundred, sometimes one hundred and fifty dollars a night in the ring. I boxed from Louisiana to the East Coast. I would get in the ring with the other guy, and we would go at it, trying to hit each other as hard as we could. The people wanted a good show, which meant bloodletting and non-stop action. In one match in Pennsylvania I heard the crowd yelling "Kill the dago! Kill the wop!" They thought I was Italian. Apparently few, if any, Mexicans lived in Pennsylvania, and in New York the same mistaken racial epithets were hurled at me. Boxing promoters in New York realized that my skills were high, and they asked if I would consider joining a professional stable of boxers. I considered this profession at the time, but I witnessed many former boxers who were "punch drunk." Scarred and broken, with little to show for their years in the so-called "sweet science of boxing," they provided a negative example for me, and I refused this possibility.

From New York I worked my way back to the West, though I took a northerly route. In Bemidji, Minnesota, I witnessed ethnic intolerance, though it was a completely alien form to me. Swedes and Norwegians, I discovered, discriminated against Finns. As I walked the streets I saw signs that read, "We don't rent to Finns" and "No Finns wanted." It was hard to believe because the Finns were blonde and blue-eyed—why would anyone be prejudiced toward them? All of the prejudice that I knew related to the darkness of one's skin. *Raúl Castro, don't feel so sorry for yourself,* I thought to myself, *they are picking on someone else here in Minnesota.* In Bemidji they viewed me through a stereotypical prism; I was a Latin from Manhattan, and somehow I must have been a great lover who played the guitar. The experience there reinforced my view that racial prejudice makes no sense.

As I continued to work my way west in the spring of 1940, I grew more astute at catching freight trains. By then I could catch a freight train that was going at high speeds with a satchel on my back. At one point I caught a passenger train from Los Angeles to San Francisco. I grabbed the accordion device between the cars and held onto it all the way to San Francisco. In another incident I caught a freight in Ogden, Utah. I always wore coveralls when I rode freight, because I wanted to remain as clean as possible in case I needed to hitchhike after arriving at my destination. When I hitchhiked I wore my letterman sweater with the three stripes on it. In those days freshmen could not play varsity, so the stripes meant that I was a three-year varsity letterman, and I found that it helped get rides. The Denver & Rio Grande freight train was about to leave the Ogden yard, and there I was, hiding behind a bush furiously trying to get on my old overalls over my sweater. Unbeknownst to me the engineer was watching, and he hollered at me, "Son, don't worry. You don't have to hurry. I'm not going to leave you. I'll wait until you get ready and then I'll start." I thought, *He must be a father. He must have a son somewhere in the same predicament.* I was grateful to him. When I was ready, he blew the whistle and started the train moving westward to its destination in Los Angeles.

We arrived at six P.M., and the police greeted the freight train; they were searching for hobos and vagrants. Vagrants, if arrested, were incarcerated for fifteen days in the Lincoln Heights jail. Men scattered like rats fleeing a sinking ship. I jumped off the train and landed in a hole that was a garbage pit. It was dark, and I couldn't see much of anything. The police chased people all over the place and forgot about me. I remained in the pit for forty-five minutes until everyone left and all grew quiet. Then I emerged from the pit, dusted off the garbage, removed my coveralls so my letterman sweater showed, and started hitchhiking again. If I had been caught and put in jail that night I never could have become a lawyer or held public office.[5]

During that time on the road I worked in the fields as a farm laborer, in addition to boxing. While harvesting spinach crops in northern California one of my fellow laborers told me that there was money to be made in the sugar beet fields in Idaho and Montana. I was told they paid seven dollars an acre to trim or clean a beet field. I thought I would make my fortune. I was young and energetic and thought it was nothing to take care of one acre of land. I arrived in Montana and was hired. The growers gave me a short hoe, and I began a routine of twelve-hour days. Most of my efforts were directed at thinning weeds. Much to my chagrin, that first day I finished less than half of an acre. It was back-breaking work, and I labored alongside Filipino and Mexican women. Despite the hardship, I continued to work in the sugar beet fields.

After a couple weeks the foreman came over to me and said, "Castro, we've got to fire you. We can't use you."

"Why?" I asked.

He responded, "We have a commissary store here, and you haven't used our commissary. We have women for rent, and you haven't rented any women. We have marijuana you could buy, and you haven't bought any marijuana." I told him that I wasn't interested in their store, their prostitutes, or their marijuana. All I wanted was to make a little money and send some of it home to my mother. So they fired me. I hopped a freight train to Oregon and began working in the sugar beet fields there. I then received a call from my younger brother, Ernesto, who followed my example and was attending college in Flagstaff.

He said that he was quitting college because he thought it was a waste of time. He said, "Raúl, look at you. You graduated from college with a good record, and now you are a bum, a hobo, working in the fields. I don't need a college degree to do that. What's in it for me if I graduate?" Ernesto's comments affected me greatly, and I realized I could not serve as an example that encouraged my brother to drop out of college. I told him I planned to return to Arizona, and meanwhile he should remain in school. He agreed, and I caught the first freight to Arizona.

When I returned to Arizona in the spring of 1941 I found a more encouraging and hopeful employment environment. Whether events in Europe or regional economic developments, due in part to military armament and federal spending on facilities in Arizona, related to this new and favorable set of circumstances, I grew optimistic about my chances to find a good job. My two-year odyssey riding the rails, boxing, and laboring in the fields, while educational, affirmed in me the notion that I was destined to achieve bigger things in my life. I applied for a job with the US State Department at the American Consulate in Agua Prieta, Sonora, located right on the border, just across from Douglas, Arizona. I took a test and interviewed with Raymond Phelan, the American consul in Agua Prieta. He hired me. Consul Phelan liked the fact that I was completely bilingual, had a college degree with a high cumulative grade average, and was enthusiastic about working for my country. I was by no means a full-fledged diplomat, but I had a special passport certifying me as an employee of the US Foreign Service and the US State Department. I remained there for five years, from 1941 to 1946. Not only did I finally find a satisfying, stable job, but Ernesto followed my advice and completed college with a teaching certificate in 1941. He taught for his entire professional career, first at Beaver Elementary School, then Flagstaff High School, and finally at Coconino High School, all in Flagstaff, Arizona.

My consulate job differed from most. I spoke with bankers, merchants, and leading business people in Agua Prieta. Each day I headed to the local bank to learn the daily foreign exchange rate, how much was available in fiscal reserves, employment conditions, and overall economic conditions in the area. Then I prepared memos for Consul Phelan, who distributed the information to appropriate authorities. Cattle brokers also came to the consulate seeking information on where to purchase Mexican cattle. Finally, much time was devoted to immigration matters. In time, I knew almost anyone of significance in Agua Prieta, and local business leaders asked me to join the Rotary Club. I was only twenty-five years old at the time, but these local leaders took an interest in me, and I joined. I was the only American member of the Agua Prieta Rotary Club, and they elected me secretary. My role in the club enhanced my role at the consulate because I had my finger on the pulse of every aspect of the border economy.

With the declaration of war on December 8, 1941, I signed up for the draft like everybody else. But the government—particularly the US State Department—viewed my role on the border as essential and issued a waiver from military service despite my experience in the army national guard. In essence, the federal government concluded that my job served the national interest more effectively than my serving in the military.

During my five years at the consulate, my workday ended at five P.M., and I would usually end up with Ben Williams Sr., a major businessman in the area. We headed over to the Gadsden Hotel in downtown Douglas and talked over drinks and food.[6] Williams, whose life and career were tied directly to the famous San Bernardino Ranch, owned by Texas John Slaughter, was scion of an old, southeastern Arizona pioneer family. Arizona senator Barry Goldwater declared that "Ben F. Williams Sr. should be part of the biography of the West." His son, Ben F. Williams Jr., like me, grew up in Douglas. Ben Jr. became an attorney, served as mayor of Douglas, treasurer of the Arizona State Bar, and served on the board of directors of the Arizona Historical Society.[7] Ben Jr. and his family have become lifelong friends and supporters, and our personal and professional histories are inextricably intertwined. My warm friendship with Walter and Mitzi Zipf also benefited my professional career since they opened the door for me to write articles about Agua Prieta in the *Douglas Daily Dispatch*.[8] The Zipfs were pioneers in the area north of Tucson.[9] Walter's brother Henry, an attorney, became my good friend. Later, he became my law partner and, though we had opposing political views, we grew to be like brothers and have been good friends for our entire lives.

The main offices for the American Consulate in this region of the border were located at Ciudad Juárez, across the border from El Paso, Texas. Periodically the consul general from Ciudad Juárez came to Agua Prieta to inspect our consulate. At one inspection in which the entire staff was in attendance, the consul general, William Blocker, asked to speak with me. He said, "Please don't misjudge my remarks. I am not being harsh, and my comments are not hostile toward you. I want to help you. I have seen your reports, and I'm very impressed with them. You have some ability, but I'm afraid you are wasting your damn time at this consulate. The truth is that you were born in Mexico of Mexican parents, and you did not go to Harvard, Yale, or any Ivy League school. You will not go anywhere working for the State Department, and I feel I owe it to you to let you know."[10]

At that same time, just to have something to do to stay occupied, I taught Spanish at the local YWCA. Many people, including the mother of the mayor of Douglas, attended these free classes. One student, David Wolfe, was in the air force and sometimes he joined me after class to have a drink or a cup of coffee. I told him that I was concerned about Consul General Blocker's comments. David responded that he was about to be discharged from the air force and he was heading to law school at the University of Arizona. He said, "Raúl, you ought to go there with me." I hesitated because I thought my mother still needed me, even though others were still in the house and helping with her care. By this time, however, I had done a lot of protection work for American GIs from the air force base and nearby Fort Huachuca who had gone across the border, drunk too much, and were incarcerated in the Mexican jail at Agua Prieta. My job was to go to the jail the next morning, interview them, make sure their human rights were not violated, and that they received fair treatment in the Mexican municipal judiciary. I became well-acquainted with Mexican attorneys and courts, and through this aspect of my job at the consulate I developed an interest in the law. David Wolfe continued to press me about the notion of law school, so I went home and discussed it with my mother. She said, "Look son, whatever you do it's going to be your decision, but I want you to go. It's an improvement. You go to school. You get more education." I made the decision in late August 1946 to attend law school; a choice that altered the professional arc of my career and reconfigured my life.

In seven short years, I transformed myself from a drifter on the rails who boxed to make ends meet, to farm laborer, to consular service worker. I regained professional momentum, made good friends in journalism and the professional world, and worked with the business community on both sides of the border with relative ease. To the north, in Tucson, a small but powerful Mexican middle class had emerged and successfully resisted the overt discrimination that characterized the lives of Mexicans in Phoenix. Tucson, I knew from my migrant work experience, did not attract the floating population of Mexican farm workers who harvested crops in and around the Salt River Valley. That situation notwithstanding, I moved to Tucson in 1946 with my eyes wide open; the city still maintained an economic structure that subordinated its Mexican residents. Between 1860 and 1940 the proportion of Anglo blue-collar workers in Tucson dropped from 67 percent to 36 percent of the total Anglo workforce thus indicating a strong upward thrust in economic mobility. The proportion of Mexican blue-collar workers declined only slightly during the same period, from 82 percent to 71 percent, thus indicating that most Tucsonenses lived in barrios, held low-paying jobs, and sent their children to schools that sought to "Americanize" them by denigrating their culture and punishing them for speaking Spanish on the playground as well as in the classroom. At the time I moved to Tucson, just after the cessation of hostilities in World War II, the public school system was an instrument of subordination rather than advancement, tracking Mexican students into vocational classes and discouraging them from attending college. As one prominent Tucson friend recalled, "It was a terrible waste of brainpower." I intended to take a different track and buck that trend.[11]

# CHAPTER V

## THE LAW

Applying and gaining acceptance to law school in the immediate post-war years differed entirely from today's process, which requires high academic achievement, competitive LSAT scores, and three or more letters of recommendation to a selection committee. Nevertheless, my path, unique compared to most, had its share of blind obstacles to overcome, disappointments, and no small amount of luck. I compressed an enormous amount of life, learning, study, and work into each day between the fall of 1946 and the spring of 1949. As the new decade dawned, I emerged as a private attorney with a practice in Tucson, Arizona.

In the first week of September 1946 David Wolfe and his new wife, Jean, accompanied me on the two-and-a-half hour drive from Douglas to Tucson. I had little money and no place to stay. After scouring the *Arizona Daily Star's* classified ads, I found an inexpensive place owned by some nuns at Third Street and Seventh Avenue, seven blocks north of downtown Tucson. I rented the screened-in porch on the front of the house, and David and Jean rented one of the apartments in the house.

Next I headed to the student employment office at the University of Arizona (UA). Dr. Victor Kelly, whom I had met in Flagstaff, headed the department, and I told him that I needed a job. "I want to go to law school," I told him, "but I don't have the funds. Can you help me get a job?" He ignored my résumé and college transcript, stated that there were no openings, and that I should seek employment at the Mexican Consulate. I replied, "Dr. Kelly, I'm not a Mexican citizen. I'm an American citizen. I've got no business going to the Mexican Consulate. They help Mexicans, not Americans."[1]

Disgusted, I left his office and went directly to the liberal arts building where I met with Dr. Richard A. Harvill, who was the dean of liberal arts.[2] I audaciously told him, "Dr. Harvill, you have a fine Spanish Department, but it can be improved, and I can improve it for you."

He looked at me quizzically and said, "What do you mean?" I replied that his teachers had Ivy League degrees and were very capable people, but, since none of them were native speakers, they had difficulty conveying to the students some of the subtle nuances of the regional dialect and accent. I told him that I could teach Spanish in his college so the students spoke with the correct accent. He said, "Young man, you are awfully confident. How can you prove it?" I reached in my pocket, took out my college transcript, and gave it to him. He looked it over, reviewed it for a while, then looked at me and said, "One of my Spanish teachers just got married last week, and she is not going to be here. I've got to have a teacher by Monday to start this semester. Can you do it?"

Scarcely disguising my surprise and excitement, I said that I could. He secured a standard contract, which I signed. I left the building, and as I was walking back toward the student union I passed Dr. Kelly.

I said, "Dr. Kelly."

"How are things, Raúl?" he asked.

"Fine. You and I are now colleagues. I just got a teaching job at this university. Here is a copy of my contract." He was thunderstruck. "Dr. Kelly," I said, "you never even looked at my credentials or asked about my qualifications. All you saw was a Mexican kid."[3]

After securing the job at UA, I walked to the law school and sought information about formal admission. In the foyer I met another young student, Hayzel B. Daniels, an African American who grew up in Nogales, another border town sixty miles west of Douglas. He too was applying to law school, and he was fluent in Spanish. We smiled at each other and struck up a conversation in both of our "native" languages for awhile and wished each other good luck. I learned that his father was one of the Buffalo Soldiers at Fort Huachuca, and we became great friends in law school. Daniels became the first African American attorney to practice law in Arizona, and the African American Bar Association in Maricopa County was later named in honor of him.[4]

My academic qualifications for law school were sufficient, but when I sat for my personal interview with the dean, Byron McCormick, he said, "I understand you have a teaching job at the university." I confirmed that information, and he calmly stated that I could not go to law school while I had a job. He added, "The law is a jealous mistress, and one cannot attend law school while holding down a full time job. It cannot be done. Furthermore, it has been my experience as dean that Mexican young people do not do well in law school. They all seem to flunk out. So I can't let you in."[5]

So I left the building and called Dr. Alfred Atkinson, who was the president of UA. I told him that I had a contract to teach at the university, but I was considering canceling because I was there to go to law school, and

Dean McCormick refused to let me in because of the job. I added that Dr. Harvill in liberal arts needed someone to teach Spanish, he was depending on me. President Atkinson called both deans. Dean Harvill confirmed his teaching need, and Atkinson told Dean McCormick to accept me at the law school. I was to receive no favors, and if my work foundered I was to be cast out. President Atkinson allowed me the chance to teach Spanish and attend law school at the same time. Due to my teaching schedule, I could not take law courses in the normal order. So I took third-year courses in my first year and in my third year I took first-year courses. Though such a schedule was intellectually challenging, I persevered, even taking courses during the summer. The rigorous schedule enabled me to complete law school in two-and-one-half years instead of three.[6]

Henry Zipf attended law school at the same time, though he was a third-year law student in 1946. Compared to me, Henry was wealthy; he had a Model A Ford. He lived a few blocks from me, and each morning he stopped by my apartment and gave me a ride to school. We became great friends, and, though he graduated prior to me, our friendship endured.[7]

Although acceptance to law school in 1946 was considerably easier than today, many more students flunked out of school; only about one-third of those who started law school with me went on to graduate. Dean McCormick, who was less than gracious in stereotyping me in our initial interview, was correct in his statement that law is a jealous mistress. For most of us the law school experience was all consuming. Most lawyers, if they were serious students, studied from early in the morning until late at night each day, with only Saturday evening for recreation. The majority of my legal colleagues were single when they went to law school, and for those who were not, the curriculum's time requirements put great stress on their marriages.

I am unsure how I completed law school while holding down a full-time university teaching position. I worked hard and recall spending all of my time either in law class, briefing legal cases in preparation for class, preparing and teaching Spanish classes, or grading papers and tests. Saturday nights provided me with few diversions from this grinding schedule. Henry and I each had only about a dollar to spend on Saturday night, so we headed to south Tucson because we could get beer there for only ten cents a glass. That was our recreation.

In the summer of 1949, I faced the new challenge of making a living as a lawyer. John Favour, one of my good friends at law school, hailed from the old territorial capital in Prescott and was a member of one of that community's most influential, prosperous, and revered families. He asked about my plans, and all I could tell him was that I did not want to return to Douglas.

Relaxing after graduation
ceremonies at the University of
Arizona School of Law, 1948.
*Photo courtesy of author.*

He suggested that I remain in Tucson, but I admitted that I had no money, and I needed to pay rent in order to hang out a shingle. John looked at me, reached into his pocket and said, "Look, here's five hundred dollars. Pay me back whenever you are able." In due time I repaid his generous loan, and he refused to accept any interest on it.[8]

With that five hundred dollars I was able to rent a house at 199 North Church Street in Tucson. The house had three rooms. The front room served as my law office. I placed a bookcase in the room and filled it with books; not law books, simply any kind of books so people might believe I was a learned person. When someone asked if I had read all of those books, I said, "yes." I slept in the back room, and the middle room was a kitchen with an icebox. Ice was delivered every day, and my icebox was always full of beer, and so my home and office became sort of a meeting place for lawyers. After work or on Saturdays lawyers from all over town parked in the lot in back of the building, drank beer, and talked about almost anything. I recall some of Tucson's most accomplished attorneys becoming regulars at my office: William Frey, Richard Fish, and Ed Morgan among them. The strong sense of camaraderie among lawyers in those days was palpable.

The shingle from that first office still exists and hangs in my home. John Favour found a fraternity paddle with the handle cut off in the garbage somewhere, and he brought it to me to use as a sign. In gold leaf I had printed on it:

## Raúl H. Castro
### *Attorney at Law*

Like many lawyers in those days, I started off receiving food as payment for my services. One Mexican lady would pay me in tortillas, another in tamales. I was single and living by myself, so I appreciated the good food. An Italian lady, who spoke English with great difficulty, asked me to represent her in some legal matter. I was relatively fluent in Italian, so I accepted the case. One day she brought me a live chicken as payment. Somehow, the chicken escaped its enclosure and ran all over my office, creating havoc and leaving feathers all over the place. On another occasion she brought me a dozen eggs. I also used this barter system of collecting legal fees when I ate at restaurants. At lunch in the late 1940s and early 1950s, waitresses often asked family law questions. I received payment for my time and legal expertise; when I ordered a hamburger, they brought me two for the price of one. This informal system of collecting legal fees showed that Tucson was not too far removed from its pioneer past.

Eventually the legal income improved, though the public image of rich lawyers with no financial worries was far from the truth. From 1949 to 1950 I had no secretary, I typed all of my briefs on an old typewriter, and when I headed to court I locked the door and placed a sign on the door that read, "Gone to courthouse, back in a few minutes."

When Dave Wolfe graduated from UA Law School I took him in as a partner, and the firm of Castro and Wolfe was established. As we put it, "We might eat turkey one day and feathers the next, but we will do it together." His wife worked as our secretary, though she received no pay. Dave and I were partners for about four-and-a-half years—from 1950 until January 1955, when I was sworn in as Pima County attorney.

Practicing law in Tucson was an education in and of itself. I grew professionally and personally as I established lifelong friendships and became aware of the lawyer's role in society, which included public stewardship and community service. Teaching at UA, graduating from law school, and entering private practice prepared me for the next stage of my professional journey.

# CHAPTER VI

## PIMA COUNTY ATTORNEY

In the early 1950s Tucson was a small city, yet increasingly urban and busy. Its population of one hundred and twenty thousand made it the most important city in Pima County and the second-most populous metropolitan area in Arizona. I enjoyed Tucson, southern Arizona, and the rich cultural amenities available in the "Old Pueblo."[1] Practicing law in Tucson was rewarding and exposed me to all types of people: rich, poor, noble, and nefarious. I was also satisfied with my personal life while I was in Pima County. I relished time with my friends and family, as well as my time spent working, but as I entered my mid-thirties my mother kept asking me "When are you going to get married?" I deflected the inquiries with humor or lighthearted banter, but I finally moved, almost imperceptibly, into the realm of matrimony.[2]

My marriage, which has lasted fifty-four years, was the most important event of my life. My wife is the former Pat Norris, and she grew up in Wisconsin where her father was a banker at the First Wisconsin Bank in Milwaukee. After her father died, her mother, who had very severe emphysema and asthma, moved to Tucson in an effort to ameliorate her illnesses. During the Korean War, Pat lived in Tokyo, Japan. She was married to William Norris, a young air force lieutenant from Lewiston, Pennsylvania. Lieutenant Norris lost his life in Korea and left Pat with two little girls, Beth and Mary Pat, who never got to see their father.[3]

Pat and the girls left Japan and visited Pat's mother in Tucson. Pat immediately secured a secretarial job with the assistant postmaster, N. L. Pritchard. Shortly thereafter, US marshal Ben McKinney offered her a job as a Deputy US Marshall, and she accepted the position. Pat provided security in the federal courthouse; she transported federal prisoners from the county jail to the courthouse, and then to the federal prison in West Virginia.[4] At that time I was in private practice and also held the position of deputy county attorney. On my daily rounds I picked up my mail at the post office, and then I went to Litt's Drugstore on the corner of Congress and Scott Street across from Jacome's Department Store. One day I noticed this beautiful, blonde woman sitting at the other end of the counter from me, drinking her coffee. I could see her in the large mirror behind the counter, and we smiled at each other. Over the next few days I slowly moved down the row of seats, until one day we were sitting next to each other. I worked up my nerve and said, "Hello," and we started talking.

Then one day in 1951 Chris Cole, a television announcer and reporter for the *Arizona Daily Star*, stepped into my office and said, "I'm having a steak fry at my house in the Tucson Mountains. Could you escort Pat Norris to the party?"

"I'd love to do that," I responded, and that was our first date.

We then dated for three years, and whenever the subject of marriage came up I avoided it. I thought I was a lifelong bachelor: I had gone to law school, I was happy, and I wanted to get ahead. I thought marriage could derail my long-term plans. Eventually, however, I realized that Pat was the one, and I planned to ask her to marry me. One of my clients was a jeweler, and I asked that he and Pat come to my office. He brought several rings, and Pat looked them over, picked her favorite. We were married in a small ceremony in Tucson.

We realized that we could not live in the little house where I practiced law and neither of us owned a car. So as a young married couple with modest incomes, we decided to look for a house and a car. After much scrutiny, I purchased a Pontiac, and Pat and I began looking for a house in our new car. Finally we located an eight-acre parcel with a wonderful house on it at River Road and Dodge in north Tucson. I hesitated, but Pat loved the place, and we bought it. We made a down payment, financed the rest, and over the years we put a lot of work into that home. Our neighbor, Gilbert "Gibby" Ronstadt, gave us several peacocks as an anniversary gift and they subsequently reproduced relentlessly and almost overran the property. Our land became an animal farm where we raised not only peacocks, but also horses, chickens, and other animals. Another neighbor, John Raskob, visited often with a young artist, Ted DeGrazia, who later became a world-renowned painter.[5] We owned that home for many years and enjoyed every minute there. We sold it for substantially more than we paid, and I remain pleased that Pat talked me into buying it in 1954.

I enjoyed horseback riding at the River Road house and property. In the spring of 1957 I rode my favorite horse, Paloma, on River Road, which paralleled the Rillito River, a lovely east-west watercourse that flowed at intermittent intervals. As Paloma trotted past the neighborhood handyman,

Pat and one of our Irish wolfhounds at our Tucson home.
*Photo courtesy of author.*

the loud noise emanating from his tractor spooked the horse, and I was un-ceremoniously bucked to the ground. I landed awkwardly and immediately knew that I broke my shoulder. A few days later, as I recovered and grew used to the cast and bandages, I took a bath. The bathtub, however, had very high sides. I became stuck. I had locked the door, so immediate assistance was not available. Pat suggested calling the police or an ambulance, but I could not justify calling in emergency personnel for my embarrassing situation.

The bathroom had a small window above the toilet, but the house was old, and the window had been painted shut for years. My wife worked on the window for about an hour and she managed to open it about four or five inches. Though she could not squeeze through the small partition, her five-year-old daughter Beth could wriggle through the opening. Head first with Pat holding her feet, Beth crawled through the window and onto the toilet. She hopped down and opened the bathroom door.

Meanwhile I had only a washcloth to cover myself, and I kept telling Beth not to look in my direction. Pat burst into the bathroom, but the challenge of lifting a two hundred-pound man out of the tub was daunting. She could not move me, and she dared not grab my arm as the broken shoulder had just been set. We struggled for two hours as I tried to turn over to my good side, and Pat tried to pull me free. I maintained a degree of dignity, and eventually I was able to get to my hands and knees and extricate myself from the tub.[6]

There are many other humorous accounts from our early years of marriage, and most illustrate some of my more pronounced character flaws and weaknesses. Each year we attended the Knights of Columbus charity dinner where they held a raffle for an automobile. Someone always talked me into buying a one hundred dollar ticket, a steep sum in the 1950s, so this particular year Pat and I were determined to avoid purchasing one. Prior to the dinner I avoided raffle ticket sellers. As we walked into the Pioneer Hotel dining room, Jack Arnold, a lawyer who later became a judge, approached us and said he saved one last ticket for me. Courage failed me, and I bought the ticket. Luckily I won the raffle, and I was the proud new owner of a Chevrolet Corvair.

As the dinner guests dispersed, everyone congratulated Pat and me, and I broke away and headed to the car as Pat chatted with some of the departing revelers. Pat told one of her friends waiting at the hotel entrance, "You watch, Raúl will probably be so preoccupied that he will come around the corner and drive right by here without stopping and just go home." As I drove home I kept thinking that I had forgotten something, and then I realized that I forgot to pick up Pat. By that time she knew I could be absentminded when I was preoccupied.

In 1954, the same year Pat and I married, I ran for the office of Pima County attorney.[7] In the 1950s the county was small enough that I could maintain my private practice with my partner David Wolfe while serving as deputy county attorney from 1951 to 1954. I worked with two Pima County attorneys during those years: Bob Morrison and Morris "Mo" Udall. Udall, of course, went on to become a superior court judge, congressman, and candidate for President in 1976.[8] As the 1954 elections approached,

County Attorney Udall called us together to announce he intended to run for Congress, and he would not seek re-election as Pima County attorney. He added that he didn't want us to seek the county attorney slot because he wanted his friend, Ed Larkin, to run for the position. I did not disguise my displeasure, and after Mo finished I walked briskly back to my office. Shortly thereafter he knocked on the door and said he wanted to talk. I cut him off, informing him that I intended to run for Pima County attorney.[9] In the end, Gordon Aldridge, another deputy county attorney in our office ran in the Democratic primary, not Ed Larkin.[10] I won the primary handily, and I defeated the Republican nominee, Bill Richey, by less than 100 votes in the general election. My friends nicknamed me "Landslide," but I defeated Bill again in 1956—by a significantly more comfortable margin—for a second two-year term.[11]

In the mid-1950s, the Pima County attorney had a much different job compared to today's county attorney. There were only four divisions of superior court and no commissioners. Today, Pima County maintains over thirty divisions and at least twenty full-time commissioners. During my tenure, the county attorney tried all major homicides; I was in the courtroom every day of the week, and the public expected it. I had a police radio in my car, and my call letters were "CA1" for county attorney. Unlike today's more administrative types, I was a hands-on prosecutor.

Sometimes I received a call at two A.M. about a homicide, and I headed to the crime scene to meet the pathologist. He would often want to go home and do the postmortem examination later because, as he would say, "it was obvious that the victim was shot." I insisted, however, that the pathologist conduct the autopsy immediately, because I had to be in court the following month proving the cause of death. To state that the victim was shot was insufficient; I had to eliminate all other possible causes of death such as asphyxiation, poisoning, drug overdose, or heart attack. Our offices required testing for contents in the stomach, blood, and various organs. At one point during my service as county attorney, I traveled to Johns Hopkins University and took a seminar on proving the cause of death. It sharpened my abilities in the courtroom and enabled me to more efficiently prosecute criminals.[12]

I had numerous interesting cases as Pima County attorney, but one stands out as memorable and fascinating largely because of the science involved in gaining a successful guilty verdict. The case involved a young university coed who gave birth and dumped the fetus in a garbage bin behind Coconino Hall on the University of Arizona campus. One of the university professors, a rare stamp collector, came upon the fetus as he looked for discarded envelopes and stamps. It was important to know whether the fetus began to breathe prior to its death. If it did, we would have a murder. On the other hand, if it did not begin to breathe on its own it would have been considered an abortion. Another element that shaped the case was that the fetus had a pair of women's panties tied around its neck.

I hired a pathologist from New York City as an expert witness and spent a week working with him. He demonstrated that the alveolus in the lung tissue had opened, indicating that aspiration had occurred, and the baby had breathed. The young woman had committed a homicide, though I convicted her of the lesser offense of manslaughter.

In another case my wife helped me locate an important witness. A Tucson municipal jail inmate committed a homicide; he killed an African American man with a baseball bat while they were incarcerated together. One of the eyewitnesses, a Tohono O'odham man, had been released shortly after the incident. I needed to locate this eyewitness, and after much searching I had him in my office. His testimony was critical to the prosecution of the case. Unfortunately he was homeless and an alcoholic, and it became quickly obvious that he had not bathed in six months. Worse, when he arrived at my office for an interview, he had vomited all over his clothes and smelled terrible. Nevertheless, I informed him that I wanted him in my office at a certain time on the day he was to testify. He failed to show. The trial proceeded, and fortunately the defense counsel, Ed Morgan, made several motions that took up a great deal of time. At the end of the day, Pat, who was then a sheriff's detective, drove me to the various homeless camps in and around Tucson. We arrived at one vacant lot on Twenty-Ninth Street, and I told Pat to stay in the car and keep the radio channel open so we could call in case anything untoward took place. It was a cold winter evening, and I saw fires all over the vacant lot. I moved around to see if I could find my witness. I finally found him, and he was drunk. I told him in a threatening voice, "Look, you were supposed to be in my office at ten this morning, and you failed to show. I want you in my office in the morning no later than nine-thirty and sober, and if you don't show up I am going to have you in jail for a long time."[13]

The case was the first superior court case for my deputy, Mary Anne Reiman (who would later become Mary Anne Reiman Richey), and I oversaw and guided her as she prosecuted her first homicide case. Though the case was unusual and atypical, she handled the situation well. My troubled, alcoholic witness appeared at the appointed time, and we called him to the stand. He was filthy and smelled bad, as usual, and the witness chair was close to the jury box. The Pima County Superior Court had no air conditioning in those days. I knew that the jury would have a difficult time concentrating on the testimony due to the unpleasant odor, so I asked the judge if I could approach the bench. I suggested that he turn on the fan and open the windows because of the smell. He replied brusquely that he was running the courtroom and told me to proceed with my case. A few minutes later, however, I noticed that he instructed the bailiff to act on my suggestion because the smell had become overpowering.

Meanwhile the defense counsel, Ed Morgan, sat, legs sprawled with his feet sticking out from underneath the counsel table. He wore some horrible orange-colored shoes, which attracted my attention every time I looked around or moved in the courtroom. He also had very large feet, which not only distracted me but also everyone else in the courtroom. It seemed that everyone would rather look at Ed's shoes than pay attention to the testimony. Maybe that was part of his defense strategy. In the end the defendant was found guilty of first-degree murder, and everyone was pleased to get out of that courtroom. As a side note, Ed Morgan has been a dear and close friend for fifty years, and Mary Anne Reiman Richey ultimately moved on to become a superior court judge and a United States District Court judge.[14]

I thoroughly enjoyed these four years as Pima County attorney. I married Pat, developed a public profile as a prosecutor and public servant, and began working more closely with Democratic Party insiders—like Tucson's power broker, Evo DeConcini and his talented sons, Dennis and Dino. I learned much more about police work, forensics, effective prosecutions, and working with my legal colleagues on both the prosecution and defense sides. Running and winning two campaigns for Pima County attorney enabled me to cut my teeth in the world of electoral politics, and I began to think about future challenges. After two terms I looked to take the next step in the twin worlds of law and politics.[15]

# CHAPTER VII

## SUPERIOR COURT JUDGE

In 1958 I decided to run for judge of the newly created Fifth Judicial Division of the Pima County Superior Court. The most difficult aspect of this campaign took place early in the race, shortly after I decided to seek the judgeship. Mo Udall, my old boss in the county attorney's office, came to me in May 1958 and tried to convince me not to run. As I had done earlier in 1954 when I decided to run for county attorney, I calmly informed him that I had already started to organize my campaign and said that if he wanted to be judge then he should run against me in the Democratic primary. If he won, that was fine. He decided not to run, and I ran unopposed in the Democratic primary of 1958.

At the time judges ran for their office like politicians, and I never grew comfortable with the process of electing the judiciary. The election of judges in Arizona was rooted in the state's Progressive to Radical origins. In many ways, the Arizona constitution exemplified the high point of Progressive political reform during that remarkable era (1890-1920) which produced great national leaders like Theodore Roosevelt, Robert La Follette, William Jennings Bryan, and countless others who brought new ideas into the arena of self-government.[1]

On June 20, 1910, president William Howard Taft signed the Enabling Act, which authorized the Arizona and New Mexico territories to draft a constitution in order to be considered for admission into the union. Arizona's last territorial governor, Richard Sloan, immediately called for the election of fifty-two delegates to a constitutional convention, and with a Progressive labor coalition dominating that important gathering, the new state forged a constitution that provided for initiative, referendum, and recall of elected officials, including judges, who were also elected by popular vote. Because Taft viewed the recall of judges as a threat to the integrity and independence of the judiciary, his administration delayed

Arizona's efforts to gain prompt admission to statehood. Taft persuaded key congressional leaders that giving such a power to the voters was irresponsible, and he refused to accept Arizona's proposed constitution until at least the recall of judges was removed. A core group of political pragmatists in Arizona agreed to modify the constitution to comply with Taft's wishes, and subsequently Arizona was admitted as a state on February 14, 1912.[2] Voters, however, issued the conservative president a strong rebuke shortly thereafter and quickly passed an amendment to the state constitution restoring the recall of judges.[3]

I had no primary opponent and ran against Robert O. Roylston in the general election. I ran campaign ads in the newspapers, placed signs around Pima County, and spoke to various groups. At a meeting of the Young Democrats on October 14, 1958, I outlined my views on how I would approach the judgeship. "All I ask is to elect me to the job I have been working at the past eight years. The county attorney represents the judges on different writs before the superior court. If elected, I'll call them as I see them. . . . No favors," I began, emphasizing my experience in the county attorney's office. "When a judge gets a 'hot potato' he calls in an outside judge. Does a county attorney call in an outside county attorney?" I asked the one hundred plus gathering. "If I am elected judge I will not call in another judge on a hot potato case. I can guarantee you that I have my training in handling hot potatoes." I ended with a flourish: "It doesn't make any difference if you are my friend or enemy, your case will be tried the same."[4] I also appeared on a televised debate with my opponent, and the moderator asked me when I was naturalized as a US citizen. I shot back that the question was not relevant to my qualifications as a judge. "I am forty-two years old," I stated firmly, "and have lived in Arizona for thirty-one years and six months. My forefathers were here before anyone thought of Arizona."[5]

On the day before the election, November 3, 1958, I ran an ad with my portrait and the tagline, "108 Attorneys of Pima County Endorse Raúl Castro." The names encircled my picture. Pima County's legal establishment— Joseph Cracchiolo, Clague Van Slyke, F. Edwin Larkin, Stewart Udall, Jack Arnold, Jerry Sonnenblick, among others—lent their reputations to support me.[6] On election day I garnered 25,059 votes to Roylston's 22,710. I issued a brief statement to the press: "I am certainly grateful to the voters for the support they gave me. I feel it is one of the greatest honors to confer upon a person to be a judge. I am looking forward to a very successful term. I have much to learn but I'm willing to give what I've got."[7]

I was sworn in on January 5, 1959. My mother and two of my brothers and my sister drove up from Douglas. Judge Lee Garrett presided, and each of the other judges, along with Henry Merchant, president of the Pima County Bar, my former partner David Wolfe, and dear friends Ashby Lohse, and James M. Murphy made kind statements about me. The ceremony impressed upon me the virtues of personal experience, patience, fairness, and humility. Presiding Judge Garrett apologized to my mother that he did not speak Spanish so that he could state to her directly what he was saying about me. She was seventy-eight years old at the time, and I introduced her to the gathered dignitaries. She stood and said in Spanish, "Judge, it's true that I don't understand a word you're saying, but by looking at your eyes and your expression I know you're saying nice things about my son." This immigrant woman and patriotic American was very proud that day. I wished my father, who had read the newspaper to me when I was a child, could have been there. I thought, *Only in America could something like this take place.*

I had little time to relish the ceremonies and the afterglow: I had to go to work. Judge Herb Krucker scheduled a jury trial for me at ten that morning. As the installation ceremony ended, I entered my judicial chambers, donned my new robe, and looked out upon the courtroom where Ed Larkin and Bob Lesher, two lawyers with whom I had worked over the past eight years, were arguing a case; my first as a judge of the Pima County Superior Court. The situation intimidated me, but that first day of hearings went well, and soon what at first seemed daunting fell into a pattern and became routine.

I served for nearly six years as superior court judge in Pima County (1959-1964), won reelection twice, and during that time I served about three years as juvenile judge.[8] I heard juvenile cases twice a week, and the other three days I heard regular cases at the downtown chambers.[9] As a juvenile court judge I had all types of minors appear before me. They had few legal rights because my years on the court were prior to the *Gault* decision.[10] Usually there were no lawyers, no rules of evidence, and no legal procedure as in adult court. The probation officer, the child, perhaps the family, and I appeared in the courtroom. Thirty to forty cases a day came before me, and I served the role of surrogate father or patriarch rather than a judge. I had to do what was best for the youngster.

Tough, streetwise youths—often Mexican, African American, or poor white children—who often had the attitude that the world was against them, appeared before me. Many told me that they held little hope, so there was no point in going to school or obeying the rules. I would look down at them from the bench and say, "What do you think I am, English or Swedish? You think I come from a rich Anglo family? I was born in Mexico of poor immigrant parents," I told them. "I picked cactus fruit in the desert for food when I was a child, and I've worked in the fields. But I worked hard, went to school, and improved myself. Today I am a judge. You can do the same." I told them that they had to stop feeling sorry for themselves, attend school, and work hard to overcome whatever obstacles they encountered. I realized that the hardened juvenile offenders respected only one thing: toughness. The fact that I was an ex-professional boxer, actually looked like I had been in the ring for hundreds of rounds, and spoke to them in candid, often vivid, terms had an impact, and through the years fewer of these types of juveniles appeared before me a second time.

Middle- and upper-class offenders posed different judicial and psychological challenges. Typically this youngster's parents were professionals, busy with their careers, and I could discern that he was left alone and felt ignored. I often discovered these children had few limits and even less discipline. If I raised my voice or got tough with this kind of juvenile defendant, I could scare them too much. My approach was milder: "Do you love your mother?"

"Yes," he would say.

"You tell me that you love your mother, yet you steal something. Don't you know that what you have done hurts your mother? It embarrasses her in the community and makes her ashamed. Is that what you want to do to your mother?" This appeal to family often worked with these kinds of children, and many times parents and children grew closer and paid attention to each other after probation and community service had been completed. Serving as a juvenile court judge was the most stressful and difficult work I encountered, and at the end of the day I would head home hoping I made the right decisions for these young people and their families.

One juvenile case caused me great internal conflict. A young woman from Minneapolis, whose parents had died and left her a lot of money, often loitered on Main Street in downtown Tucson. Bars, saloons, and nightclubs were the businesses of choice in that part of town, and she would meet and attract men, then take them home for all night parties. She had son whom she exposed to these activities. I received a petition to sever her parental rights. Another aspect of the case was that she and her child were Anglo, and the men she brought home were exclusively African American, and the evidence revealed that all had either been convicted of felonies, like burglary, drug possession, or assault. I analyzed the evidence, considered the overall situation, and severed her parental rights. I noted that the only people she exposed her son to were convicted felons; all had been convicted of crimes such as burglary, drug possession, or assault. I realized that my decision might appear to be based on racial considerations and that

I could suffer attacks from the media, but there was no public reaction to what otherwise could have been a very controversial judicial rendering. The case bothered me, however, because it looked like I had acted contrary to my views concerning breaking up a family based on racial considerations, although I knew that I had not in this specific instance.

The regular judicial calendar had its predictable criminal, civil, and probate cases, and I heard them at least three days a week. When I was not a juvenile judge I would hear these cases five days a week. We rotated this calendar every six months so a particular judge would hear criminal cases for six months, then civil cases for six months, then probate cases for six months. The system worked as all of the judges I worked with remained intellectually and emotionally engaged in our respective cases.

I realized that the bar—working as an attorney—was more interesting than serving on the bench. As a lawyer I created a framework for my argument and decided how I would most effectively prove my case. In most cases I had three or four elements to establish, and the fascinating part was organizing the foundation for my argument. On the other hand, a judge plays a reactive role, making sure that everyone follows the rules of procedure and evidence and that the jury receives proper instruction. That dimension of the judicial system is repetitive and overly predictable. The jury, not the judge, except in divorces or equity cases, decides most case in the superior court. For the intellectually curious person like myself, the bench can be somewhat tedious and boring.

Another major responsibility for a judge is sentencing, and, though various guidelines existed when I sat on the bench, I always tried to demonstrate care and wisdom in sentencing offenders. Sentencing someone to death was especially difficult. I concluded that if I had sentenced someone to die I must maintain the fortitude to witness the execution. In these few instances I drove to the state prison in Florence, Arizona, entered the outer office of the death chamber, and watched the procedure. Even though I knew that the person committed a heinous crime and did not deserve to live, the process bothered me, and I found it extremely difficult to internalize.

Sometimes during my tenure on the Pima County Superior Court the serious bordered on the comedic. Pat and I had a horse farm on our eight acres on River Road in the foothills of Tucson. By the late 1950s we had about forty Shetland ponies, Hackney ponies, Arabian horses, thoroughbreds, peacocks, chickens, and Irish Wolfhounds. The place was an animal menagerie, akin to a zoo. In 1958 Pat entered four of our ponies in competitions at the Yavapai County Fair in Prescott, and one of our stallions,

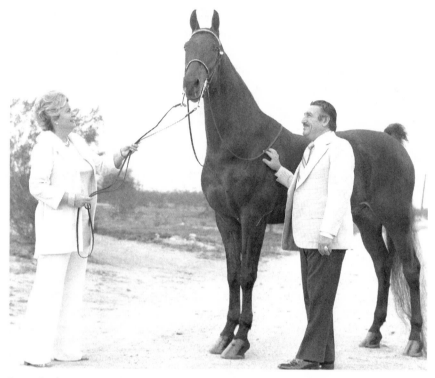

Pat and I showing one of our prize winning horses at a show in Louisville, Kentucky, 1976. *Photo courtesy of author.*

with the cumbersome name of Atkinson's Hillswicke Blue Boy, emerged as the grand champion at that prestigious competition.[11] Running the farm with various competitive breeds of ponies required a lot of work on the weekends. Pat usually had a long list of jobs for me, and on Saturday mornings she taped it on the refrigerator. One particular weekend I had to paint the white rail fence that surrounded the property. I slipped into my Levis, boots, old shirt, and sombrero, grabbed the paint cans and began painting the fence.

After an hour, a green US Customs Border Patrol car approached and cruised to a stop. Two patrolmen exited the car, and in grammatically flawed Spanish they asked to see my papers and green card. I politely told them that I had no papers and no green card. They grew aggressive and surly in their language, and I could tell that they were ready to arrest me. Finally they asked, "For whom do you work?"

"The lady of the house," I answered. Like most husbands, I did not willingly volunteer to go out there and paint the fence; she recruited me to complete the task.

Then they asked how much she paid me, and I replied, "Nothing, but she allows me to sleep with her." That lighthearted response elicited greater anger, and I realized that I had to diffuse the situation. I said, "Wait a minute. Can't you see that sign in front of that gate? It says 'Castro Pony Farm.' Well I happen to be Castro."

Then one of them said, "Are you Judge Castro?"

"Yes, I am," I said. The confrontational mood changed quickly, and after a thousand apologies they left. While comical on the surface, the situation hurt my feelings, and I realized that sometimes society took one step forward and two steps back.

I encountered the same kind of racial and cultural intolerance on another occasion at the Greyhound Bus Depot in downtown Tucson. I often drove there to meet relatives visiting from Sonora. In this instance I wore Levis, boots, and a straw hat, and I could see four Border Patrol officers approaching me from two sides to interrogate me. As always, I showed

Campaigning with Arizona senior senator Carl Hayden, 1962.
*Photo courtesy of author.*

them identification. It bothered me. When Pat and I headed to Phoenix on judicial matters and we had to stay overnight, we learned that I had to stay in the car while she registered for the room. If I attempted to rent the room there would be no vacancy.

Partway through that final term as Pima County Superior Court judge, I grew increasingly restive and looked for greater challenges. The 1960s were a time of change, and though I had achieved more in my life than I could have imagined, I knew there was more to accomplish. I looked more carefully than ever at statewide elective office and noted that Arizona's political culture had shifted over the past ten years. In 1962, for example, eighty-four-year-old US Senator Carl Hayden, the dean of the US Senate who had represented Arizona in Congress since statehood, won a hotly contested campaign for reelection against arch-conservative Republican Evan Mecham. Hayden was a legend and—though he defeated Mecham 199,217 to 163,388—the margin was the smallest in his distinguished career. Mecham's surprisingly strong showing anticipated the dramatic changes that would shape Arizona's political culture in the next four decades.[12]

I knew something significant had taken place in that election, and in a broader sense this fundamental transformation—the increasingly conservative political posture in Arizona in particular and the American West in general—contrasted markedly with the early twentieth century political mood reflected in the Radical politics, Unionism, and Progressivism that marked my father's years in the mines and in the communities of southern Arizona. I spoke with Senator Hayden and his chief of staff, Roy Elson, after the election, and they told me that when Hayden entered Congress in 1912, fifty years earlier, Arizona embraced unorthodox political bromides, Populist insurgency, and radical political ideas such as women's suffrage and allowing voters to legislate directly. Hayden supported these political reforms. But the old, "Radical" West had become conservative before my eyes. Certainly Arizona in the early 1960s began to identify with conservative Republicanism, entrepreneurial capitalism, and so-called traditional values. I mused that the Hayden-Mecham election in 1962 vividly captured this Radical-to-conservative drift that had taken place in the region's electoral politics and political culture, and I pointed to Senator Barry Goldwater's upset of incumbent senator Ernest McFarland ten years earlier as the first manifestation of this shift in political culture. I needed to figure out where my history and future fit into statewide politics. Fortunately when Lyndon Baines Johnson won the presidency, and his good friend Senator Carl Hayden was in his second year in his last term in the Senate, the political stars aligned, and I received the chance of a lifetime.[13]

# CHAPTER VIII

## AMBASSADOR TO EL SALVADOR AND LBJ

As I sat in my home on River Road in March 1964, I received a phone call from someone identifying himself as Roy Elson. "Do you remember me?" he asked.

"Sure," I replied. Elson was a former Spanish student at the University of Arizona, and I knew that he was now US Senator Carl Hayden's chief of staff. As chairman of the appropriations committee, Senator Hayden was one of the most powerful members of Congress. Hayden, eighty-seven years old, relied heavily on Elson, imbuing him with a great deal of political influence.

Elson asked if I was interested in becoming United States attorney for the district of Arizona. I said, "Well, Roy, I think you have made a mistake. I'm not interested in being US attorney. I'm already a superior court judge, and I see that as a more prestigious position. Besides I have already been Pima County attorney. My idea has always been to move forward, so I can't accept that position."

He then asked what kind of appointment interested me, and I quickly replied, "An ambassadorship." I briefed him on my consular service in Agua Prieta, explained that I was familiar with the skill sets required of a diplomat, and urged him to seek an ambassadorship for me. He grew quiet, then said that perhaps an ambassadorial appointment could be arranged and to expect to hear from him in the near future.

What prompted this call? In the 1964 election cycle, Roy Elson, who won the Democratic nomination for the US Senate seat vacated by Senator Barry Goldwater in his ill-starred campaign for president, sought my support in his race against Governor Paul Fannin, who won the Republican primary for the US Senate seat. Naturally I supported Elson, but he lost a close election to Fannin. He tried again to win a seat in 1968 only to lose in his second attempt, this time to Goldwater, who reclaimed his seat four years after his bruising loss to Lyndon Johnson in that famous 1964 presidential race.[1]

After my phone conversation with Elson, Senator Hayden called and asked if I would consider serving as ambassador to El Salvador. I said that I would, so Hayden called President Johnson, told him he had a favor to ask, and placed my name before him. Johnson said he knew me and recalled a political rally in Tucson in 1960 where we campaigned together. Johnson raised the issue of my name and expressed concern that people might confuse me with Fidel Castro's brother and Cuba's minister of defense, Raúl Castro. Johnson, always the politician, feared that this potential misidentification might cost him some votes.

Hayden called, explained the problem, and said that the President wondered if I would consider changing my surname to my mother's maiden name, Acosta. My exasperation was evident to Senator Hayden. I told him the American people were not ignorant; they could differentiate between the Cuban defense minister and me, and I would not abandon my father's name. If I had to change my name then there was no reason for me to serve as an ambassador. President Johnson finally relented, and I began the deliberate process of Senate confirmation, though Hayden's influence among his colleagues shortened the length of the review of my qualifications to a significant degree. In fact, at one point during my confirmation hearings Senator William E. Proxmire had to be reassured by the chairman of the Latin American subcommittee of the Committee on Foreign Affairs, Wayne Morse, that I was "not related in any degree whatsoever to the Castro in Cuba."[2]

When Senator Hayden informed me that the administration planned to put my name forward and that the notion of moving to El Salvador was real, I had mixed emotions. The excitement of a new adventure coupled with profound change in our lives created a combination of optimism, fear, and sadness. Pat and I loved the River Road property and all of our animals, and suddenly we faced the prospect of parting with them, selling or renting the property, and leaving for Washington, DC, to meet with State Department officials and protocol officers. In the fall of 1964 we began the inexorable process of leaving Tucson and moving to El Salvador.

On October 1, 1964, the Senate Foreign Relations Committee confirmed my appointment as ambassador to El Salvador. I was forty-eight years old when I prepared to say goodbye to Tucson, Arizona, and my friends throughout the state. Much to my surprise, my friends—about four hundred of them from Douglas to Flagstaff to Phoenix—held a large going away dinner and celebration for me at the Ramada Inn in Tucson. I received a host of tributes and awards, like the American Medal of the Daughters of the American Revolution, and plaques from the City of Tucson and the City of South Tucson. Dean Francis A. Roy of the University of Arizona

College of Liberal Arts, a French instructor when I taught Spanish in order to get through law school, said, "My first memories of our ambassador were of a dapper young instructor on the campus with a much sharper moustache than now." Roy Elson, seeking votes during the last month of his general election campaign, commented on his role in securing my appointment, adding, "Raúl Castro will make us proud."

I was asked to speak and said, "We all feel we have a mission in life. My mission will be to promote a better understanding between Latin Americans and this great country." It was a memorable evening, and Pat, the girls, and I enjoyed every minute of that tribute in Tucson.[3]

As we prepared to head to Washington, DC, and then to El Salvador, Pat wondered about her role in an embassy. She envisioned an idle time and countless hours relaxing on the front porch of a big house. As an active and self-sufficient person, the notion horrified her, but we soon discovered that her duties required several skills and much work. I left for Washington on October 25 while Pat remained in Tucson for two weeks, selling the horses and other animals, renting the house, and taking care of all other details requisite for relocation. Then she arrived in Washington to attend the US Foreign Service Protocol School. Angier Biddle Duke, whose family donations created the endowment for Duke University, oversaw the school, and Pat took some elementary Spanish classes. After these classes she returned to Tucson, picked up our daughters, who had just completed their fall semester in school, and together they flew to Miami to join me on our first leg to El Salvador.

My diplomatic background enabled me to streamline, even avoid, "ambassador training" at the US Foreign Service Protocol School. Since I spoke Spanish and knew the internal administrative processes, I received a briefing and recent history of the embassy in El Salvador, thus avoiding several weeks of drudgery. I knew, for example, that in each embassy there was a career foreign service officer, the deputy chief of mission (DCM), who oversaw daily operations of the embassy and assisted the ambassador on nonpolitical matters.

When we arrived in El Salvador's capital, San Salvador, we were met by the DCM, various attachés and diplomats, and driven to the ambassador's residence, which was a huge French style mansion. The staff of twelve greeted us, and I marveled that at home in Tucson I painted the fence, fed the animals, cleaned the yard, and washed the car. This was a different world and required substantial adjustments.

We plunged into the diplomatic life of long hours, many demands, and seemingly endless social obligations. At first Pat, who spoke only a smatter-

The United States embassy residence in El Salvador.
*Photo courtesy of author.*

ing of Spanish, had trouble communicating with our well-meaning staff, none of whom spoke English. So Pat, along with four twenty-two-year-old marines, attended Spanish class. She studied deep into the night, and though her seat alongside the student marines raised some eyebrows, she soon spoke Spanish quite well. At the same time she embraced her other obligations with alacrity, taking appointments, planning menus in advance, and appearing at social functions.

Early in my tenure, on May 3, 1965, a 7.5 Richter scale earthquake struck San Salvador and literally rocked the entire coastal country. The quake, which lasted about one minute with aftershocks for weeks thereafter, killed at least 125 people and injured five hundred. The main road to Ilopango Airport was cracked as was the main runway, rendering it virtually useless for weeks. President Julio Rivera declared a state of emergency as flooding and electrical blackouts followed on the heels of the tremors. It was a serious event, and I had to respond quickly and brief not only the American authorities but also the Salvadoran authorities on rescue operations.[4]

The tremors shook us out of our beds at about five A.M., and Pat, who was sleeping in a bedroom next to the girls, awoke to their screams and the sounds of furniture sliding across the floor. Glass broke, walls cracked, and

Family portrait with Pat, Beth, and Mary Pat, 1965.
*Photo courtesy of author.*

finally Pat made it out of bed and to the top of the staircase. She shouted to the girls that they had to get out of the embassy as the branch candelabra fell and candles and debris littered the floor. At the reception room entrance at the bottom of the stairs hung a large crystal chandelier, and Pat expected it to fall at any moment. When she and the girls reached the bottom of the stairs they hugged the wall, skirting the chandelier as they went around the reception entrance to the large front doors and outside.

The ground shook as the Salvadoran guards steered Pat and the girls away from the embassy grounds because they feared the huge gargoyles might fall on top of them. In the meantime, Pat looked around and asked "Where is the Ambassador?"

No one had seen me in all of the confusion. It was a very warm night, and I had slept in the nude. As the quake began, I could not get to my pajamas. The sight of the American Ambassador to El Salvador running through the embassy in the nude and out into the streets was not the image I wanted to convey to the Salvadoran or the American public. As buildings crumbled around us, I finally found some clothes and came down from my upstairs bedroom. Fortunately everyone at the embassy survived the frightening event, and Pat, the girls, and I slept on an outside porch for two weeks, trembling whenever one of the aftershocks knocked us off balance. The beautiful old residence was so unstable that the government moved us to a new residence in San Benito, in the northern part of San Salvador. The new residence had a pool and therefore met with the girls' approval.[5]

My mission in El Salvador was three-fold: improve US-Salvadoran relations (and relations with all Central American countries), discourage Communist infiltration, and expand US trade and economic development (with El Salvador in particular and the other countries in the region in general).[6] The fact that I spoke Spanish cemented relationships and facilitated open

With President Lyndon Baines Johnson in El Salvador, 1964.
*Photo courtesy of author.*

dialogue with the middle class, political elite, and the military. During my ambassadorial stint in El Salvador, trade between the US, El Salvador, and the surrounding Central American countries improved dramatically. El Salvador's economy grew at an average of 6 percent annually during my four years there, and trade among the five Central American nations (El Salvador, Honduras, Nicaragua, Costa Rica, and Guatemala) increased during the same period, from $69 million to $220 million annually.[7]

On July 7 and 8, 1968, President Johnson visited El Salvador to attend the Central American Summit in San Salvador. This curious televised venture marked one of the highlights of my ambassadorship.[8] Johnson became the first US president to visit all five Central American countries on one trip, and he received an unexpected and enthusiastic welcome from the Salvadoran people at a time when his popularity in the US and throughout the world had dropped precipitously.

Indeed, Johnson's two-day visit to El Salvador was complicated and controversial. It was initiated by several invitations issued at various times by individual Central American presidents following Johnson's meetings with them at the Punta del Este Conference in April 1967, and from Costa Rican President José Joaquín Trejos Fernández during his visit to the White House on June 4, 1968.[9] Beyond the implication of these entreaties, by late 1967 the Johnson administration recognized the need to rekindle US interests in Latin America as a whole, and Central America in particular.

Much had changed since Johnson assumed the presidency on November 22, 1963. Johnson replaced Kennedy's Latin American appointments, and Thomas C. Mann became the single most important person directing the Johnson administration's Latin American policy. Mann believed that private investment and the private sector held the keys to economic development in the western hemisphere and that the US should assume a neutral stance on other reforms. Following Mann's advice, Johnson de-emphasized social reform programs and reduced pressure upon military governments for democratization. To combat Communism in the western hemisphere Johnson continued Kennedy's military assistance programs, but by 1967 the US Congress concluded that some governments had overspent. In some cases US aid was promoting the continuation of military dictatorships. Over the next year, Congress and the president battled over the amount of military assistance to Latin America.

Meanwhile, Vietnam overwhelmed the Johnson administration. He fought rear guard actions at home in an effort to save his "Great Society" domestic programs and faced increasing amounts of racial and urban violence. Discussions within the Johnson administration about improving Latin

American relations culminated in February 1968 with several important policy decisions. These included a smorgasbord of initiatives: a message by the President to the Inter-American Cultural Affairs Council; a vice presidential trip to South America; an invitation to the presidents of the Latin American countries to participate in the Hemisfair in San Antonio, Texas, scheduled for May 1968, after which Johnson would host them at his ranch in nearby Johnson City; invitations to four Latin American presidents for official visits at the White House; a meeting between Johnson and Mexican President Gustavo Díaz Ordaz in Mexico; and a Johnson interview with selected Latin American journalists. Over the next two months the President's advisors reviewed various possibilities regarding visits to Latin America by the President, Vice President, Mrs. Johnson and others.

Johnson and his advisors initially considered a trip to South America and, in early May, envisioned that the trip include a short stop in Central America. As White House advisors pondered the Latin American junket, the five Central American presidents were planning their own meeting, though they had yet to agree on a time and place. Johnson's advisors saw an opportunity to meld the two meetings together. National Security Advisor Walter W. Rostow proposed that the US could force the issue and combine the meetings to fit Johnson's schedule. Secretary of State Dean Rusk, Assistant Secretary of State Oliver T. Covey, and Latin American Advisor Thomas C. Mann favored trips of short duration largely because of US domestic considerations. The recent assassination of Robert F. Kennedy, coupled with continuing urban unrest, prompted these men to urge caution and suggest that Johnson remain out of the US for only a short period.[10]

Other top advisors saw advantages for a meeting in Central America. They focused on San Salvador as the most likely meeting spot because it presented the most favorable security situation. Covey pointed out that San Salvador offered the President an opportunity to visit a public school named after him and an Agency for International Development (AID) educational television station that originated with Johnson-supported program funding in 1967. Rostow suggested that a mass at San Salvador's Cathedral in memory of Robert F. Kennedy would "set a high tone for this and subsequent meetings." Johnson concurred and appeared anxious for the Central American trip to materialize. "Hurry [and] get this thing rolling," Johnson scribbled to Rostow on June 7, 1968.[11]

On June 8, 1968, White House Chief of Staff Bill Moyers called and said that the President wanted to come to El Salvador next month for a Central American Summit where he could meet with all the presidents of the Central

American countries. My job was to make the arrangements, oversee the process, and assure a positive outcome for all of those in attendance. I contacted the various presidents and informed them that the President planned to arrive in El Salvador to meet with them. Interestingly, each president, Oswaldo López Arellano of Honduras, José Joaquín Trejos Fernández of Costa Rica, Julio César Méndez Montenegro of Guatemala, and Anastasio Somoza Debalye of Nicaragua had to receive permission from their respective parliaments to visit El Salvador for the summit. El Salvador's President, Fidel Sánchez Hernández, served as host.

I contacted President Montenegro of Guatemala to begin the planning process. He said, "You know, Mr. Ambassador, I am having a great deal of trouble with communist guerrillas up in the mountains along my border with Honduras, and I don't think I can spend time out of my country right now. I have got to get rid of these guerrillas as they are giving us a lot of trouble."

I said that Guatemala City was only twenty minutes from San Salvador by air force jet, and I could have US Air Force jets fly him and his wife; they could have breakfast at home in Guatemala City, fly to San Salvador for the day, and fly back to Guatemala City in the early evening. With that arrangement, he agreed to attend.

Then I called President Oswaldo López Arellano in Tegucigalpa. He was an air force general, and he spent time in Tucson as he trained at Davis-Monthan Air Force Base. I knew him well. I telephoned him and said, "Mr. President, this is Raúl Castro calling you, and I would like to invite you to come and meet the President of the United States here in San Salvador."

He replied, "I can't do it. My country is at war with your host country, El Salvador. We are fighting each other, and there is no way that I can leave my country and visit enemy territory under these circumstances. It just can't be done."

I said, "Mr. President, you won't be visiting enemy territory. You will be coming to the Organizacion de los Estados Centroamericanos (ODECA); the ODECA building is partially owned by your country, therefore you won't be entering enemy territory, but you will be coming to your own country. I don't see how you could be viewed as a traitor for coming into your own country."

ODECA, created in October 14, 1951, was designed to promote regional cooperation, integrity, and unity in Central America.[12] Each country contributed part of the funding for the ODECA building in San Salvador, and all five countries maintained offices there. It was a lot like the United Nations building in New York City, with its international neutral jurisdiction. I convinced him and he agreed to attend.

After that I called the President of Nicaragua, Anastasio Somoza Debayle, and told him that, on behalf of the United States, I would like to invite him and his wife, Hope, to San Salvador to meet and talk with President Johnson.[13] He asked if the President of Costa Rica was going to be there, to which I said "yes." Like the others, President Somaza announced several obstacles for not attending. He told me his father had been murdered as a result of a conspiracy formed in San Salvador, and he was not on speaking terms with the president of Costa Rica, José Joaquín Trejos Fernández. I scrambled for some ideas and invented some reasons why he should attend the meeting. Foremost among them was that the President of the United States requested his presence, and he intended to accompany him to the Catholic church.[14] I assured Somoza that he had no fear of harm, and I falsely added that the President of Costa Rica would not come to El Salvador. In the end, he agreed to come to San Salvador for the summit.

I finally contacted President José Joaquín Trejos Fernández of Costa Rica and invited him to the summit. Not surprisingly he said that he would not go anywhere Somoza went. I assured him that they would not be in the same place at the same time, and after some salesmanship I finally persuaded him to come up to San Salvador. I had convinced and cajoled all of the Central American presidents to come to a meeting with President Johnson.

One week prior to the summit, about ten students in San Salvador protesting the Vietnam War demonstrated and burned Lyndon Johnson in effigy. Student protests were not uncommon at this time as the youth throughout the world expressed their profound disagreements with LBJ and his Vietnam policy. The Salvadoran students were no different.[15] The university was only two blocks from the embassy, so the small number of student protesters attracted media attention. Bill Moyers called me and told me that President Johnson was cancelling his trip. I immediately contacted the White House and advised that a cancellation could have serious and negative consequences. President Johnson responded to my admonition at midnight. I told him that he was perfectly safe and the protesters numbered only in the teens. He insisted that he wanted his safety guaranteed, and I again assured him that he would be safe.

I said, "Mr. President, there is no way you can cancel the trip. I have invited every president, all of whom have agreed to come to the meeting at great sacrifice to many. It would do irreparable harm to our international relations with them for us to just arbitrarily cancel the meeting after I insisted that they come and told them how important it was. They would feel like we treated them like puppets on a string."

Earlier the State Department and I advised the President that El Salvador was a politically stable country that held five consecutive free elections during the 1960s, and as a result of the legislative and municipal elections of May 1, 1968, President Hernandez had strengthened his control over the government. I reiterated that the country continued to enjoy a high rate of economic growth, increased private investment, had new foreign credits, and public investment programs financed by international assistance and increased tax revenues. [16] He calmed down and the meeting was reinserted into his calendar. The presidential visit received the "green light" on July 1, 1964, so there was little time to prepare, and the itinerary provided little if any time for serious discussion of the issues. LBJ and his advisors knew that since 1963 the Central American states experienced relative prosperity thanks to the high sales for their coffee and cotton in the world market and a 600 percent increase in inter-regional trade; from $69 million in 1963 to $220 million in 1967.

The five Central American presidents arrived in El Salvador on July 2, and by the time Johnson arrived five days later much of the work of the meeting had been completed. This portion of the summit was a success; the regional common market represented a move toward self-sufficiency and economic integration that President Johnson and his administration hoped to see duplicated in Latin American countries and throughout the world. In fact, after the first session the five presidents issued a declaration expressing concern over possible restrictions by more developed countries against Central American exports and urging that their countries jointly pass a tax on imports into Central America. Each president also issued statements supporting the aforementioned economic integration of the five coffee and sugar republics faced with large foreign trade deficits. [17]

There were a few back-stories that framed President Johnson's visit. I met each of the Central American presidents at Hopongo Airport upon their arrival. When López Arellano of Honduras arrived, instead of taking him to the ODECA building as I had promised, we headed to the US embassy. He protested and accused me of treachery. I assured him that I was his friend and said that I was taking him a back way to a side entrance to the embassy so that no one would know he was there. I told him that Fidel Sánchez Hernández, the President of El Salvador, was there, and I thought they should talk. A smoldering dispute had divided these two leaders and their countries, and I took the opportunity to put them in the same room to discuss their differences. I gave them a quart of scotch, escorted them into a room, and told them that they should discuss the problems between El Salvador and Honduras. "Resolve these differences,"

I admonished, "because war is not good for either country and it is in both of your interests to end the dispute."

After about two hours, the bell rang and they were ready to see me. They had resolved the issues between them and settled the problem. Honduras agreed to release forty Salvadoran soldiers imprisoned for more than a year after they allegedly blundered over the Honduran border. In return, El Salvador agreed to release a convicted Honduran-born bandit that the Hondurans claimed was illegally arrested across the border. Since the transboundary dispute was resolved, I telephoned the head of the El Salvadoran parliament, which was in session and awaiting word. They were told by their president that the matter had been settled, the stalemate was over, and peace had been restored. The two parliaments subsequently worked out the agreement, and we then had a big reception in celebration of peace. This was a move that cleared the way for a productive summit.[18]

Another problem, minor compared to the Salvadoran-Hondoran tensions, centered on President Samoza of Nicaragua. A huge painting of him hung in the ODECA offices, and three of the presidents objected to it. By resolving this dispute—staff removed it from sight during the meetings—the presidents were able to sign the joint declaration on the Friday night prior to the arrival of President Johnson.

Before the President's landing in San Salvador, however, an emissary from the State Department contacted me and requested that I guarantee a large, favorable crowd at the airport when Air Force One touched down. He said that they wanted ten thousand to one hundred thousand people there cheering for Johnson. He added that the President was kind of low, and his request was actually an order. "He's depressed," the State Department official told me, "because everywhere he goes he gets booed because of Vietnam, and he needs something to fortify him."[19] I told him that I could accomplish the task, but it would cost money. He asked how much, and I told him ten thousand dollars. He said that they could only afford six thousand dollars, and he reached into his pocket and pulled out six thousand dollars in greenbacks and gave them to me. He obviously came prepared to pay for the good public image. Apparently these funds were available to reimburse El Salvador for extra expenses incurred on security measures.

I met with the general of the national guard, the most cohesive and powerful military organization in the country. I told him that I needed 100,000 people at the airport to cheer President Johnson when he arrived at the airport in San Salvador. I requested barefoot peasants in torn shirts and straw hats that carried signs, some misspelled, saying, "Viva Johnson." He responded that he needed about ten thousand dollars; I took out the six thousand dollars, gave it to him, and we struck an agreement. When LBJ emerged from Air Force One at Ilopongo Airport, thousands of Salvadorans cheered, yelling, "Viva Johnson." American network television picked up the live feeds and this portion of my mission was accomplished.

In the limousine Johnson turned to me and commented in a sincere voice, "They really like me here don't they?" President Fidel Sanchez Hernández of El Salvador accompanied the President and me in the first limousine while our wives and Luci Nugent, the Johnsons' daughter, were in the second. Anti-war demonstrators created mischief, and we took a few detours to avoid the protestors. Students distributed leaflets urging people to "decorate" Johnson's face with eggs, and they carried placards referring to the summit as "The Dragon and the Five Mosquitoes."[20] Headlines in the US media declared "LBJ Car Target of Paint Bombs," and "More than 2000 Jeer 'Murderer of Vietnam,'" but these overstatements sold papers rather than reflect the truth of the situation in San Salvador that day. We arrived unscathed at the embassy residence, and all were safe and happy.

THE WHITE HOUSE

WASHINGTON

July 30, 1968

Dear Mr. Ambassador:

Thank you, once again, for the cuff links you presented to me on my departure from San Salvador. I will treasure them always as a symbol of our Nation's friendship with San Salvador and as a memento of an historic and fruitful visit there.

With warm appreciation and every good wish to you and Mrs. Castro,

Sincerely,

The Honorable Raul H. Castro

Thank you letter from President Lyndon Baines Johnson. Note that he mentioned the cuff links I presented to him as a parting gift. *Photo courtesy of author.*

The President and his family moved into the embassy residence while my family moved into a home next door. The President's daughter, Luci Nugent, was extremely gracious during her two days with us, and Pat enjoyed both Mrs. Johnson and Luci. Interestingly, the Johnsons refused to socialize in the evenings after official daytime activities ceased. They disappeared into the embassy residence and remained there all night.

Another oddity marked the social aspects of this presidential visit. While the presidents met at the ODECA building, Liz Carpenter, Mrs. Johnson's secretary, decided that all of the wives of the visiting dignitaries should see the historical and cultural sights of El Salvador. We rented two buses for this outing, and Ms. Carpenter told Pat that she was in charge of the whistle and should blow it to make sure all the wives and guests boarded the buses at eight-thirty A.M. the following morning. Pat expressed her dismay and told Liz that these women were wives of presidents of sovereign nations, not school children, and she would not whistle them aboard a bus. Pat discarded the whistle and instead escorted everyone aboard the buses at the appointed hour. The outing proved a great success.

Like the bus tour, an evening function at the embassy honoring Salvadoran leaders, revealed President Johnson's unusual style. The protocol officer at the embassy usually introduced each guest by name, position, and social and professional significance, but he had not been in El Salvador for years, so I played his role that evening. Thus, I stood first in line, followed by my wife, then President Johnson, Mrs. Johnson, and then Luci Nugent. The Salvadoran dignitaries stopped and talked with me, and soon President Johnson kicked me.

"Look," he said, "you are supposed to be introducing these people to me; you're not here to chat with them." He expressed his displeasure in rather pungent terms, and it became clear to me that he wanted the spotlight. So I reverted to the role of protocol officer and moved on to the next person whenever anyone tried to talk to me.

The rest of the evening went well, and the President complimented me and asked if I would consider moving to Washington and working for him in the White House. I said, "No, Mr. President, I'm a foreign service animal, and I feel I can best serve my country by being in the foreign service."[21]

At the end of his two-day stay, President Johnson pulled me aside and said he wanted to transfer me to another post. At first I thought this was a great idea and added that, after nearly five years in El Salvador, I was prepared for the next move. Then he dropped a bombshell: he wanted me to go to Bolivia.

"Mr. President," I stammered, "I don't think you like me very much

At a reception in San
Salvador, El Salvador, 1965.
*Photo courtesy of author.*

because Bolivia is a very difficult, poverty stricken country, and this looks like I'm going backwards." He assured me that my assessment was incorrect; there were a lot of problems in Bolivia (strikes, shootings, and terrorism) due to Che Guevara's activities, and he needed someone with my background and language skill in that country. Guevara was fomenting revolution, and I was the person to extend the American presence in that difficult foreign service post. Then he finished the conversation: "I want you to go. I'm sending you there."[22] He departed El Salvador and over the next few days landed at the other four Central American capitals, made statements of goodwill and cooperation, then headed back to the US where Vietnam protests and domestic turmoil consumed his administration.

To add insult to injury, before moving to Bolivia, I traveled to Washington, DC, for my orientation briefing. President Johnson called me before I left El Salvador and said that he wanted me to bring along my butler, Ovidio Wong Hoy. The request perplexed me. I informed President Johnson that Ovidio was Chinese, a very good cook, and ran a residence with great efficiency. He spoke neither English nor Spanish, however, and I wondered how he could survive away from the embassy. But Johnson insisted on this curious request to bring Ovidio to the United States.

A few weeks later when I landed at the airport in Miami on my way to Washington, the secret service met me as I disembarked from the plane. I thought, I feel rather important being received in Miami in this fashion. But the first question they asked was whether or not I brought my butler, the Chinese man, with me. They were interested in Ovidio, not me. Apparently

President Johnson had appropriated him for service in the White House, and I was the last to learn of this development. The secret service spirited him away. In this instance, the butler trumped me in importance; he worked in the White House, and I did not.

Six months later as I walked down Pennsylvania Avenue in front of the White House, I saw White House security harassing Ovidio. I approached the security guards and said, "What are you doing to this man?" They told me that he wanted to get into the White House, but he was a security risk. I identified myself, showed my security pass, and told them that the president had personally selected him to work in the White House, and they had better call the president's office. They called and learned that he had access to the White House. That night Ovidio visited me at my hotel room and thanked me. In gratitude for my kindness he ironed my pants and shined my shoes.

Scholars conclude, and I agree, that President Johnson was a very capable president but flawed in his relentless quest for power and influence. He used political power to his advantage. This quality inhered in his personality, and I knew that I was somehow wired quite differently from the president. His two days in El Salvador, which appeared to be a successful diplomatic gambit, demonstrated that he could be charming and forceful. In some ways his Central American tour was a final grasp of political gamesmanship in an effort to appear presidential and maintain power. Soon after he returned to the US, he dropped out of the 1968 Democratic primary. Meanwhile, I headed to my new ambassadorial post in La Paz, Bolivia.[23]

# CHAPTER IX

## AMBASSADOR TO BOLIVIA

Being sworn in as Ambassador to Bolivia by Secretary of State Dean Rusk, 1968.
*Photo courtesy of author.*

President Johnson announced my nomination as ambassador to Bolivia on July 15, 1968, only one week after his trip to El Salvador and the Central American Summit. I succeeded Douglas Sheridan, who had been envoy to Bolivia since November 1963.[1] The move took me from the smallest and most densely populated Central American republic to the fifth largest country in South America. El Salvador, about the size of Massachusetts, had an estimated population of three million. Bolivia, located in the central portion of South America, was nearly eight times the size of New York state and had a population of four million. The *Yuma Daily Sun*, ran an Associated Press and the headline,"LBJ to Move Castro Up."[2] Although my appointment to Bolivia appeared to be a positive promotion, it proved to be a near-death experience for Pat and me.

Pat returned to Tucson to visit friends and family and prepare, as an "ambassadora" should, for the next post, which differed entirely from that in El Salvador. By this time she realized that things do not automatically run smoothly in the ambassador's household, and her role at a US embassy required preparation and hard work. For example, in El Salvador she once asked the cook to chop turkey giblets for a Thanksgiving dinner party and discovered—too late—that he included the bones in the stuffing. On another occasion the piano stuck shut when a noted artist had agreed to play for a group of distinguished dinner guests. Pat weathered these glitches in stride, and learned from her mistakes by researching Bolivia in order to avoid repeating errors in protocol like these. Her research also included learning more important issues about La Paz that required her attention. She secured a long bibliography on Bolivia and began her research, but a short, fifty-four page booklet, *The Post Report*, proved especially relevant, not only for her but also for me.[3]

With Beth and Pat in La Paz, Bolivia, 1968. Photo courtesy of author.

Reviewing troops at the Presidential Palace in La Paz, Bolivia, 1968.
Photo courtesy of author.

The ambassador's residence in La Paz, she discovered, consisted of two main floors, a finished attic, and a small basement. The first floor centered on a large entrance hall; on one side there were three adjoining living rooms and a small, comfortable sun porch with a spacious service area next to it. The second floor had a large master bedroom, three smaller bedrooms, three bathrooms, a sitting room, and another sun porch. The grounds were ample and beautifully landscaped and contained a gazebo in the main part of the garden. In addition to information regarding our residence, Pat also gathered essential information for the practical aspects of living in La Paz. For example, La Paz is the highest capital in the world, which made cooking times an adventure. Meats and vegetables had to cook much longer than at lower altitudes, making pressure cookers highly desired commodities. She also discovered from her research that the slippery sidewalks in La Paz required rubber heels and ripple soles to assure sound footing on the steep and narrow sidewalks. Household items like cosmetics, toiletries, spot removers, insect repellents, and drug supplies, though available in La Paz, were very expensive, and Pat advised that we stock up on these necessities.

There was more. Because of the brilliant sun, dry-skin creams, sunglasses, and suntan lotion were mainstays. Pat prepared a long list of scarce commodities: gift wrappings, greeting cards, pins, waste paper baskets, sponges, dish towels, padlocks, batteries, light bulbs, and flashlights. Her research informed her that tennis players in La Paz could not use traditional tennis balls, but had to use balls specifically designed for high altitude because the former took a heavy toll on racket strings. Calling cards, she informed me, should be purchased for all embassy personnel; a married diplomatic officer required at least two hundred cards. Pat's hiatus in Tucson helped immensely in fortifying her with useful knowledge as we approached this challenging assignment.[4]

My preparation proved more problematic. As State Department officials briefed me, President Johnson commenced a program of delay, keeping me in Washington for two months. He claimed that strikes, military revolts, and guerrilla warfare compromised my safety. I told him that since Bolivia was a Latin American country, the warfare would follow the desired schedule of those fighting—I could arrive on a weekend since the generals left the capital city for the country to visit their families or girlfriends. I finally convinced State Department officials and the White House that if I flew into La Paz surreptitiously on a Saturday, no problems would arise. The flight went as planned, and I stepped off the plane to a bullet-riddled and abandoned airport where my friend Monsignor Pio Laghi, who served as the ambassador from the Vatican, met and escorted me to the US embassy in La Paz.[5]

On Monday, like clockwork, fighting began again. Warfare was not the only problem: police, teachers, and other sectors were on strike or protesting. The internal power struggle took on its workweek-like predictability, but even though the weekend was over, I was ensconced in the embassy and felt secure. In addition to the constant political turmoil, Bolivia was unique in other ways. The State Department considered it a hardship assignment and made it only a two-year venture. The La Paz airport sat at 14,000 feet above sea level, with the city 2,000 feet below at 12,000 feet above sea level. Year-round snow-capped mountains added to the stark beauty and isolation of La Paz and its environs. The fire department received calls infrequently because the altitude and lack of oxygen made starting fires very difficult. The lack of oxygen also made breathing a challenge for visitors. When Pat and I first arrived in La Paz we always kept oxygen nearby, and it took about three months for our bodies to acclimate to the altitude. We were always very cold and had severe headaches due to the altitude. During that time we awoke gasping for air at about two A.M.; we reached for the oxygen pump, placed a tube in our mouths, and breathed the precious resource. In the three-month period of adjustment, our bodies added another quart of blood to our systems. Most Americans on duty in Bolivia lost about twenty pounds during their first year in La Paz. American women who became pregnant inevitably had to evacuate the Bolivian capital because birthing a child was nearly impossible at that altitude. Another consequence of the high altitude occurred when one returned to lower altitudes. I often had nosebleeds whenever I returned to Washington, DC, for briefings because my body had to rid itself of the extra blood.

Bolivia posed personal challenges on American foreign service workers as well. Due to its remoteness, military and political intrigue, high altitude, and mountainous geography, spouses often had difficulty adjusting to the life-style. It was a different and dangerous environment. Most of the Americans stationed in Bolivia were men, and those with wives faced unusual domestic challenges. Shopping, walking, and local errands oftentimes posed obstacles of enormous magnitude, and when husbands needed to travel on work-related missions, many wives grew lonesome. On numerous occasions young wives, exasperated and alienated, packed their bags in the middle of the night and headed back to the familiarity of the United States. On the other side of the ledger, I received numerous reports of husbands carousing in the bars and misbehaving, especially if their wives returned to the US, which created pub-lic relations problems for the embassy. So, in an effort to impose a degree of social stability, I confiscated all of the wives' passports, kept them in a safe, and if they wanted to leave Bolivia they had to see me first. If they expressed good reasons for leaving other than their general discomfort—marital problems, for example—I would hand them their passport, assist them with their trans-portation to the airport, and bid them farewell. Otherwise I tried to persuade them to stay so that we avoided the innumerable problems caused by stray-ing husbands. Personnel problems existed even overseas, and as ambassador I needed to deal with them as part of my overall work portfolio.

Our residence in La Paz was actually small compared to our residences in El Salvador, and later in Argentina, which were palatial. The embassy staff, Aymara and Quechua Indians, was delightful, and by this time Pat's Spanish was excellent, so communication was no problem. Bolivia featured stunning vistas and mountains, though it remained economically challenged and the people, collectively, were quite poor. The unending turmoil made this assignment fascinating but dangerous, and a high percentage of the one thousand or so Americans attached to the embassy were military workers. My mission in Bolivia centered on reporting the revolutionary situation there; who entered the country and who left.

Early during my tenure President René Barrientos, who had risen to power through the military as an air force general, paid his respects, welcomed me in a variety of ways, and we formed a fast and cordial, yet professional friendship. Barrientos was a fascinating and charismatic leader. He even spoke the most important native language, Quechua, and developed a penchant for feats of valor that endeared him to the public. He had earned his pilot's license in 1945 and gravitated toward the reformist party, the Movimiento Nacionalista Revolucionario (MNR) which was led by Victor Paz Estenssoro, a Bolivian political fixture, reformer, and president of the country numerous times. In 1952 Barrientos flew out of the country to bring back the revolutionary leader, Paz Estenssoro, from exile once the MNR had toppled the existing regime. In 1957 he became commander of the Bolivian Air Force as a reward for his dedication to the cause. A fiercely anti-communist, pro-American ideologue, Barrientos served as his country's vice president for three months in 1964 when he was elected with President Victor Paz Estenssoro, then in a coup d'état, overthrew Paz Estenssoro, and became president from 1964 until his untimely demise in 1969.[6]

Barrientos survived numerous assassination attempts during his presidency. The eighth in a long series took place on May 3, 1965, in Cochabamba, Bolivia's second-largest city, when a man on a motorcycle fired into a jeep carrying the Bolivian president. The assailant disappeared into the night. Fortunately Barrientos was wearing a bulletproof vest, and the one bullet he took in this particular attack—in the buttocks—was not life threatening. He issued a press release similar to others when someone tried to assassinate him: "Elements opposed to the big national majority that supports the presidency of General Barrientos" were responsible for the unsuccessful attempt on his life.[7]

Just prior to my arrival in Bolivia, Barrientos and his administration experienced a serious crisis. His troubles began when Cuban president Fidel Castro published Che Guevara's diary, which he kept during his abortive guerrilla campaign in Bolivia.[8] Guevara had been captured and executed by CIA-trained Bolivian troops in 1967, and the diary, retrieved by the Bolivian military, was to be sold to foreign publishers in an effort to raise money for government coffers. Somehow Castro secured the diary, and he provided its contents to selected foreign publishers for free, undermining Bolivia's initiative. An army investigation revealed that Barrientos' good friend and interior minister Antonio Arguedas slipped the diary out of the country to Castro. Arguedas and his brother fled to Chile, where they were granted asylum, and held a press conference declaring that they were Marxist humanists and admirers of Castro. As a result of these developments, military and civil leaders met in an atmosphere of crisis in La Paz as unrest mounted against the beleaguered president. A senator was arrested, and Barrientos issued a curious statement to the press: "Rumors of a coup were unfounded. I expect the armed forces to remain loyal to me except if special circumstances intervene." In fact, Barrientos' government fell apart the night after the Arguedas revelation and the Social Democratic Party quit the four-party government, and twelve cabinet members submitted their resignations. Clearly his hold on power was flimsy at best when I entered the war-torn country one month after this scandal rocked Bolivia.

President Barrientos invited me on a number of excursions, and through his hospitality I grew more knowledgeable about the history, culture, and people of Bolivia. I took weekend fishing trips with him, accompanied him on official business, and grew to expect his calls to join him on various sorties. Though quizzical, I almost always responded positively to his invitations because, according to protocol, whenever the President issued an invitation, the Ambassador accepted. In March of 1969 he invited me to a dedication of the opening of a new bank close to the Brazilian border, near the Amazon River. I attempted to pass on this invitation, indicating that the US had no interest in the bank. He insisted, claiming it was a new concept. The native population in that region wanted to learn how to use banks, and the presence of the American ambassador could motivate them to modernize. I finally agreed to his invitation given the apparently sound reasoning. When I arrived at the airport to leave for the bank, the President was choosing a plane. He checked three different planes until he found one to his liking, and we stepped on board.

I immediately noticed that it held about twenty-five people; twenty soldiers, a pilot, the co-pilot (who happened to be the president), his aide-de-camp, and me. I remarked that the payload was too heavy at this altitude. His response, in retrospect, was amusing: "The soldiers are small, Mr. Ambassador, and they don't weigh much." After further debate, he reluctantly ordered half of the soldiers off the plane. It took a long distance to get airborne at fourteen thousand feet, and we barely cleared the adjacent mountain pass at twenty thousand feet, and then we placed our oxygen masks around our heads. Much to our horror, there was no oxygen; someone had disconnected the lines. All of the soldiers and the pilot passed out, leaving just the President and myself conscious. Fortunately we were both robust in our lung capacity; Barrientos was a big man with big lungs, and I ran track and boxed in college at Flagstaff, which was at seven thousand feet. The President succeeded in flying us to our destination, and when he landed he looked at me and said, "We almost got killed." I said, "You are right, and I don't want you to invite me ever again."[9]

President Barrientos dedicated the bank, enjoyed the festivities, and then we headed to Cochabamba to dedicate a new road from there to

Lima, Peru, which had been built with American money. That trip went well because Cochabamba sits at a comparatively lower nine thousand feet.

About one month later, on April 27, 1969, Barrientos, who seemed to be on the move constantly in an effort to refurbish his image as a Populist reformer, asked me to accompany him in a helicopter to the Cochabamba region. I refused and fabricated a story that important visitors from Washington, DC, were arriving at the embassy, and I would be indisposed. As it turned out, the helicopter crashed or exploded, depending on various eyewitness accounts, killing President Barrientos. The reality of the situation was that President Barrientos used me as a shield. He had me travel everywhere with him because he figured that his detractors would not kill the American ambassador. If he kept me close, he would be safe.

Our intelligence sources suspected an army commander, General Alfredo Ovando, spearheaded the plot to eliminate Barrientos, though the press reported the crash as an unfortunate accident. Ovando was out of the country at the time, and State Department officials preferred a civilian leader as successor, Luis Adolfo Siles Salinas, who was the sitting vice president, a professor at the university, and son of a former Bolivian president. Siles was sworn into office before the general could return to Bolivia and cause problems or take over the presidency with force. But our covert intelligence revealed that there would be an assassination attempt on the new president at a parade and ceremony at Cochabamba. He "got sick" just before the parade and did not appear. Drew Pearson, the syndicated columnist who wrote the widely read "Washington Merry-Go-Round," marveled that Siles quietly stepped into the presidency without incident or revolution: "Not a shot was fired in a country where a good many presidents have been shot or hanged in the past."[10]

Unfortunately the Siles presidency was short-lived, marred by disagreements with General Ovando. I knew Ovando harbored ambitions to become president, and he immediately began to lay the political groundwork as Barrientos' legitimate successor. But Siles and the general clashed on numerous issues, including Ovando's persistent meddling in affairs of the state. In 1969, one year prior to scheduled national elections, Siles backed the incipient candidacy of the mayor of La Paz, Armando Escobar Urias, as Barrientos' true successor. This endorsement threatened Ovando's electoral plans, and he launched a successful coup d'état on September 26, 1969, overthrowing Siles, who went into temporary exile.[11]

Pat and I had other close calls in Bolivia. At one point a guerrilla operative, who brazenly worked in the streets of La Paz, was detained and found to have instructions to kidnap the American ambassador's wife, take her to the

Brazilian border, and kill her. Pat walked our Great Dane each morning, and the plan included grabbing Pat while she was out with the dog and placing her in a nearby waiting van. Pat breathed a sigh of relief that the operative was killed the day before the kidnapping and murder were to take place. After this brush with danger and intrigue, Pat had bodyguards wherever she went in Bolivia. On another occasion, guerrillas threw bombs at our residence in La Paz. Daughter Beth, who attended the University of Texas at Dallas, was visiting for the Christmas holidays. As she slept at the rear of the residence, someone tossed a bomb over the back wall. The explosion knocked her out of bed, crumpled the wall, blew out the servants' quarters windows, but fortunately no one was injured. A group of students from a nearby university were found responsible for the incident, and Beth had quite a tale to tell her friends upon her return to school for the spring semester.

Other less dangerous, but challenging experiences marked our stay in Bolivia. Before Pat had bodyguards assigned to her, she decided to attend an event in Sucre, a beautiful mountain town and the ancient capital of Bolivia. Pat and Beth went with a tourist group and arrived at the main hotel in Sucre where the tour director, an effervescent young woman, welcomed the entourage with restraint and elegance. The old hotel, though charming, lacked heat, and due to the altitude the place was freezing. Pat and Beth slept with socks, shoes, coats, and piles of covers. They survived the night, and the next morning the group took off for an even higher location in the mountains called Oruro, a small Indian town where ancient customs prevailed among the inhabitants, and women wore bowler hats. The four-hour drive grew precarious, and with the mountain road winding in tight turns, Pat became sick. When they arrived in Oruro, the car sputtered to a halt and died. Pat was nauseated, had diarrhea, and now she had no transportation. The only bathroom in the town belonged to the Catholic priest, so they escorted Pat there to use the facility. The toilet had no water, and there was an open window where six children peered in at Pat, pointing and smiling at her. The priest finally brought her a bucket of water so she could flush the toilet. As Pat put it later, "I was the entertainment for the day."

The tour leader had to get the other people back to Sucre, so Pat's ride left without her. They made arrangements to transport her back to Sucre, but they were unusual ones. Her mode of transportation was a cattle truck that had been modified with slats to haul pigs. The pigs smelled, and Pat was wedged between the driver and an old man who neither washed his clothes nor bathed, and neither of the men in the truck spoke Spanish, only the local Indian dialect. Pat and the pigs departed Oruro, down the winding mountain road toward Sucre. Then she noticed that the driver stopped at the top of the hill, took out a shotgun, and walked off into a field. Soon he returned, slid into the truck, and continued driving. Four hours later the unlikely trio and the pigs arrived at the outskirts of Sucre where there was a police checkpoint. Pat had no passport or other identifying documents in her possession and thought she could end up in jail. The driver showed his papers as did the odiferous passenger, and the local official looked at Pat for a moment and waved them through. Somehow Pat made it to the hotel and collapsed in her cold room, happy that the mountain drive on the pig truck culminated in her safe return.

In another exciting situation, we encountered crocodiles on a lake. In Bolivia and other Latin American countries linguistic missionary groups teach native peoples Spanish. One group in Bolivia invited me to visit their camp in the jungle, and I accepted the invitation in the spirit of forging good American relations with the local peoples. Pat and I flew to a landing strip and the missionaries transferred us to a small, two-seat plane that had a slat in the rear to create room for a third person. The second leg of the journey took us even deeper into the jungle to a smaller landing strip, and there was nothing but jungle for hundreds of miles. We emerged from the small plane to very gracious Indian hosts. The men wore the bark of a local tree, and the women wore nothing. Everyone had feathers in their noses and ears. They guided us to their village, which had lots of thatched huts, and babies lying around in hammocks or crawling on the ground. They performed various dances and offered us food, which we ate, but I was not sure what we consumed. The missionaries then took us back to their camp, a wooden structure with a dining room and living quarters for both men and women. They planned a lake excursion for us, and at dusk we climbed into dugout canoes—each of which had a small motor for occasional use and emergencies—and made our way onto a very large lake.

Four passengers filled our canoe: Pat, a missionary, a man standing up with a pole to push us along and keep us away from the bank, and me. We needed to stay away from the bank because they wanted to show us the crocodiles that inhabited the shores. The missionaries shone lights toward the banks so we could see the eyes of the crocodiles. They could determine a crocodile's size by how big and far apart its eyes were on its head. We also learned that the missionaries killed them for food. At ten P.M. we decided to return to the missionary camp. They decided to use the motor, but it quit, and we were stranded in the middle of the lake. We spent the next hour yelling, being bitten by mosquitoes, and praying someone would realize we were stranded in the middle of the lake. Finally, at about midnight, a sortie motored up to us, and we were saved. Undaunted, we arose the next morning and ate our breakfast: crocodile tail. It tasted like chicken.

When we returned to La Paz I immediately took our Great Dane for a walk and passed a young woman on the street who said, "Good morning, Judge, how are you?"

"Young lady," I said, "you called me 'Judge.' You must be from Arizona. Who in Bolivia would know that I was a judge?"

The woman was born and grew up in Nogales, and she married a Bolivian diplomat. That encounter made me think of home, and, as it turned out, my time in Bolivia was limited and I would soon return home because 1968 brought a change in administration in the United States. Richard Nixon defeated Hubert Humphrey in a close, hotly contested presidential election, framed by the Bobby Kennedy and Martin Luther King assassinations as well as the continued agony of the Vietnam War.

Nixon, however, wanted to flex American foreign policy muscles in Latin America, so he and his new team of advisors formulated the "Look and Listen" tour shortly after he took office in January 1969. He sent New York Governor Nelson Rockefeller and a team of experts on a grand tour to survey conditions and help formulate administrative policy in the western hemisphere. The plans kept changing, but I learned that Governor Rockefeller and his group wanted to visit La Paz on May 31, 1969. The itinerary included visits to Ecuador and Venezuela before Bolivia, but plans were not firm. I informed the State Department that it must carefully consider its approach to this visit and that I preferred to speak directly with the Governor. He called, and I informed him that, unfortunately, the Bolivian populace identified Rockefeller with big oil company exploitation and "Yankee Imperialism." I encouraged him not to visit Bolivia. I stated bluntly that it was dangerous, and I could not guarantee his safety. He dismissed this admonition, so I suggested he visit Santa Cruz, Bolivia, along the Brazil-Argentina border. "No," he told me—he wanted to visit La Paz, President Siles, and the Bolivian leadership.[12] In the end we agreed that Rockefeller would fly to the airport at La Paz, attend a reception that featured key officials, but he would not go down to the city.[13]

As Rockefeller left the US and started his "Look and Listen" tour, protests in Peru and Venezuela erupted with such intensity that planned visits to those countries were cancelled. As one journalist who indulged in adverbs put it, the crowds were "humiliatingly unfriendly and frighteningly hazardously hostile." When he arrived in Bolivia from Quito, Ecuador, his scheduled visit had been trimmed down from twenty-two hours to three because his Ecuadoran visit produced "wild disorder" among the citizenry. The press described "Rocky's Unhappy Journey," as "a bust." I breathed a sigh of relief when I saw his plane lift off from La Paz Airport for its next destination.[14]

Welcoming Nelson Rockefeller and his wife Happy in La Paz, Bolivia, 1968. Note the secret service and military personnel surrounding Rockefeller and his wife.
*Photo courtesy of author.*

About a month after the Rockefeller visit, I received a cable from President Nixon indicating that he "accepted my resignation with regret," though I had never resigned. Nixon wanted his own people in place, so he requested copies of my tax returns; his way of ridding himself of Democratic appointees. Senator Barry Goldwater, reelected after his four-year hiatus in Arizona, spoke up for me during that time. He learned that I had mitigated the situation for oil companies in Bolivia and thought retaining me there was a good idea. In fact, I learned that at a Republican Party fundraiser at the Pioneer Hotel in Tucson, he said that Nixon was crazy for replacing me as ambassador to Bolivia. Senator Goldwater's protests fell on deaf ears; Nixon's Internal Revenue Service people found nothing wrong with my taxes, but he appointed another ambassador. Pat and I returned to Tucson where I planned to practice law. I had no idea in 1969 that I would reenter the public arena or run for elective office, but it was great to be home and to have served my country abroad.

# CHAPTER X

## GOVERNOR OF ARIZONA

When Pat and I arrived in Tucson from our service in Central and South America in the winter of 1969-1970, John Molloy, chairman of the Pima County Democratic Party, and Ed Loper, director of the Tucson YMCA, met us at the airport. Before we had the chance to gather our land legs, they began talking to me about running for political office. They discussed the US Senate and Arizona governor, but this seemed premature since I had been away from the state for nearly six years. I appreciated their respect and faith in me, but as I told Molloy that day, "I think you are crazy. I have been out of the country so long; people have forgotten about me, and no one knows me." I needed to take time to assess the political landscape and contemplate if I wanted to seek statewide office; was it time for a Mexican-born immigrant, naturalized in 1939, to run for governor or senator in a state like Arizona, which still struggled to embrace its Hispanic heritage?

At first I dismissed their suggestion, but as I traveled the state speaking to various business groups, high schools, community colleges, and labor organizations, I thought about Molloy's ideas about seeking statewide office. If I ran for the US Senate, I would face incumbent senator Paul Fannin, a former governor who had close ties to the state's business elite and reflected the Goldwater conservatism that fueled the political culture of fast-growing Maricopa County, home to Phoenix and other "pro-growth" communities.[1] Incumbent Governor Jack Williams, a former radio personality, mayor of Phoenix, and two-term incumbent, was the fair-haired politico of the conservative Republican establishment as well, and his friendly and accessible public persona ingratiated him to the status quo.[2] Both seemed unbeatable, but as I spoke to audiences in Flagstaff, Prescott, Douglas, Globe, and elsewhere during the spring of 1970, I began to reassess the validity of a run for office. On May 1, 1970, as I addressed the pro-business Tucson Trade Bureau, I informed this group of businessmen that I did not want to be a "sacrificial lamb," but I might consider a run for governor if enough interest existed in voter-rich and Republican-leaning Maricopa County. I went out on a limb and told this group that if there were sufficient interest there I would seek the Democratic nomination for governor. During the question and answer session, I told them it would cost two hundred thousand dollars to make a respectable run in the primary and another four hundred thousand to make a credible race in the general election. Raising such amounts of money, I informed my audience, would be a profound challenge.

On May 28, 1970, very late in the primary season, Dick Casey, a Tucson political columnist, for the *Tucson Daily Citizen*, hinted that I planned to run for governor. "Castro found that he has enough support after testing Arizona's climate for several weeks and will officially announce in about two weeks," he wrote in his weekly column, "he has petitions in circulation and told this writer this week that he would become a candidate. All things considered," he continued, "Castro's entry into the race is a bright spot for Democrats, even though most insiders consider incumbent Republican governor Jack Williams nearly unbeatable."[3]

I officially entered the primary campaign on June 18, 1970, the third Democrat to announce his candidacy for governor of Arizona. Mesa automobile mogul Jack Ross and Chandler mayor George Nader had announced the previous month. I issued my declaration for candidacy in three locations that day: the Press Club in the Arizona Land Title Building in Tucson, where about five people were present; then I drove to Phoenix and held a press conference at the Westward Ho Hotel; then drove alone down to Yuma and gave another press conference. At each location fewer than ten people—most of whom were my friends—were in attendance. I stated, perhaps quixotically, that the political climate was right for a Mexican American to be elected to the state's highest office.

I pledged an active campaign against the incumbent and underscored the fundamental planks of my platform: pollution control, drug abuse prevention, law and order, and improved business and cultural relations with Mexico. "First is the environment," I declared, claiming that the last legislature approved piecemeal safeguards on air and water pollution too little, too late. I planned to tackle air pollution and environmental problems head on, citing the critical need to minimize not only copper smelter, but also automobile emissions pollution. Drug abuse and education were societal problems that also required greater funding, and the missing element in this fight was a lack of leadership from the governor's office. I explained that my third platform plank was the maintenance of a lawful and just society. "I support to the last ditch the right of anyone in our society to say what he believes and demonstrate peacefully," I stated, "but I will deny with all my being the right for anyone—hippie, craftsman, or intellectual—to destroy property, commit violence on any other person, or in any way take the law into his own hands." Leadership was the answer; if Arizona had a governor who would open the lines of communication to all and make an honest effort to understand the problems of the many, the kinds of disorders the state had suffered could be minimized. Finally, relations with Mexico, particularly our neighbors in Sonora, needed to be improved.[4]

A few days after I declared my candidacy, statewide newspapers assessed my qualifications. They said that "Raúl Castro, 54, born in Douglas and one of 14 children in a poor Mexican American family, presents a different campaign image." Most reported that I had two children and travelled the campaign trail alone, using my own car and paying for my gas. They noted that I was a former boxer, miner, teacher, Pima County attorney, superior court judge, and US ambassador to El Salvador and Bolivia. In addition to my political and legal résumé they informed readers that all my life I had been fighting because people would tell me that I could not and should not do something because "I was a poor Mexican boy." I was certainly a change from the incumbent.

Williams, I repeated in my speeches, had been an unaggressive and "do-nothing governor," and I issued a challenge to my primary opponents, as well as the incumbent: "I've been a teacher and know about students and educa-tion. I've been a miner and know about their problems. I have worked closely with drug abuse problems and crime. And I have lived among the poor. I ask my opponents what they know first-hand about these problems?"[5]

The press dutifully covered other concerns. I stated that the economy—specifically inflation—was a key issue in the campaign, and an aggressive governor could fight inflation. I recognized problems with the state's welfare system and targeted welfare commissioner John O. Graham as a bureaucrat that "must go." I agreed with some progressive education re-forms, but rejected student violence and other unlawful means of protest. "In South America," I told audiences, "the students actually ran the univer-sities, even to the point of setting some of the curriculum, and it did not work." I favored greater fiscal support for the universities. I set an upbeat and optimistic tone for my grassroots campaign in the primary.[6]

My most serious challenger in the Democratic primary was colorful Jack Ross, a Mesa auto dealer and television personality. He was young (forty-two years old), the father of four sons, flamboyant, and was always accompanied by his glamorous ex-movie-star wife, Aquanetta. Together they exuded charm as they mingled with prospective voters; they excelled at small talk. Ross and his wife had been on local Phoenix television for sixteen years, co-hosting a popular program sponsored by Ross' dealership that ran old movies. He had statewide name recognition, and he ran a highly polished, slick primary campaign.[7] He made some startling statements, however, claiming that Republicans were regulating everything with computers, and if Williams were reelected, he would own the Arizona Board of Regents, "lock, stock, and barrel." He almost always attacked the other party with vigor, asserting that the Republican-controlled Arizona legislature passed unconstitutional laws, and Republicans had gerrymandered voting districts to their advantage. He touted his background as a businessman, saying "we've had enough radio announcers by the score," in a reference to Williams' background as a radio personality in the 1940s and 1950s, and asked rhetorically, "Why not a businessman?" Ross claimed that if he were nominated for governor in the Democratic primary, he would leave Williams "in the dust" in the general election on November 3, 1970.

George Nader, a forty-seven-year-old business consultant, a native of Miami, Arizona, a mining community, was a three-term mayor of Chandler, Arizona, and a veteran of World War II who was awarded the Bronze Star and Purple Heart. His wife, Dorothy, was a charming woman, and his two teenage sons were often on the campaign trail with him. I never discerned what he stood for because he would always say, "I'm neither a liberal, conservative, moderate or Progressive, but a combination of all these things." He talked about his accomplishments in Chandler and how he hoped to extend them to the state level.[8]

Perhaps the most significant aspect of my run for governor of Arizona in 1970 was the fact that I celebrated my ethnicity and heritage as a political asset. As the *Yuma Daily Sun* wrote about my speech to the Yuma Press Club on June 20, 1970, "A naturalized citizen seeking the office of governor of Arizona told the Press Club Friday that being a Mexican American was an asset rather than a hindrance."

I told that gathering that "ever since I was little, I was told 'Raúl, you haven't got a chance.' Well, I've been lots of places for a guy who didn't have a chance. It was inconceivable to the people of South America that a man born in Mexico of Mexican parents would be selected to represent the United States. My answer was that I am part of the melting pot." I continued that being bilingual was an asset, and Arizona had reached the point where it accepted an individual on his own merits. This observation, I told the Yuma audience, helped me decide to run for governor. I added that Latin American newspapers, in their efforts to distinguish me from "that other Castro," called me "Yanqui Castro." This elicited a good laugh.[9]

In Yuma, so close to Mexico, I emphasized border relations in my speeches. "Thirty years ago," I said, "I was holding conferences with Mexico on drug control. So the problem is not new to me." I stressed that US relations with Mexico must be rehabilitated and asked rhetorically, "Has the governor of Arizona been invited to Mexico for anything?" I posited that the welfare of Arizona and Sonora went hand in hand and that previous experience as the attorney for a Tucson bank taught me that a strong economic relationship with our neighbors to the south brought on huge financial benefits. "Arizonans," I stated frankly, "could care less if I were black, yellow, brown, or white, because I have support in Kingman, Flagstaff, Tucson, Yuma, and among the various tribes in the state." I said I was a fighter, and even though Maricopa County would be a challenge for me, I intended to go there to "slug it out."[10]

Arizona voters made their primary election choices on September 8, 1970. Two days prior to the election I ran ads in all the major newspapers, touting my "working man" background and my judicial, governmental, and foreign policy experience.[11] On election day I polled nearly twice the number of votes of my two opponents combined, which one daily newspaper called a "surprise victory." I received 50,729 votes; Ross, 29,112; and Nader, 25,941. My popularity in Pima County was no surprise, but my victory in Maricopa County, which according to one daily newspaper was "traditionally almost impossible for an outsider to crack," had to rate as an upset over the two other Democratic competitors in that county. Ross, who campaigned for six months and spent great sums on media, expressed extreme surprise at my primary victory but promised to support me in the general election.[12]

On September 9, 1970, I began an eight-week campaign marathon for governor against incumbent Jack Williams, who had no Republican primary opponent. Besides focusing my message on the environment, drug abuse, law and order, and greater border cooperation and commerce, I addressed other issues that the Williams administration had neglected or ignored. I faced the opposition of the most powerful newspaper in the state, the *Arizona Republic*. Its archconservative publisher, Eugene Pulliam, maintained political influence in every corner of the state, and he pledged to do everything in his power to reelect Governor Williams.[13] Pulliam's support for Williams posed huge obstacles for me in Maricopa County, but in spite of this difficulty, I continued to fight. At nearly every campaign stop I called for implementation of a state-supported kindergarten program and for free textbooks for high school students. Speaking in Spanish and English to a crowd in Douglas, I urged bilingual education and stressed how Governor Williams and the legislature cared less and less about education, not only for our grammar and high school students, but also for those who embarked on higher education.[14]

In the general election, I hit Williams on his lack of concern for the environment. At the annual Arizona Town Hall meeting at the Grand Canyon, I scarcely believed my ears at Governor Williams' response to information about certain animal species on the verge of extinction: he shrugged his shoulders and asked, "What's the difference?" In the same vein, he declared that all of the discussions about preserving Arizona's land, air, and water for future generations were just a bunch of "hot air." I had never heard such callous disregard for our natural resources, and I reported my interpretations to Kiwanis clubs, Rotary clubs, high schools, labor groups, and anyone else that cared to listen. I found it incredible that a governor could be so unaware of the delicate balance of nature and wondered how Arizonans could expect to solve environmental problems with a chief executive who refused to recognize them.

"As your governor," I told audiences, "I will continue to be what I have always been as a public servant—sensitive enough to understand the problems of our state and energetic enough to do something about them."[15] I recognized the need to bring the state prison system into the twentieth century, and I also raised questions about the dog- and horse-racing industries. If elected, I intended to seek an immediate investigation into rumors of wrongdoing in pari-mutuel racing. Though the incumbent met with the attorney general early in 1969 about the rumors, the results of the meeting were not revealed to the public. Problems in these industries raised issues of organized crime in Arizona, and I intended to address it immediately upon assuming office.[16]

Two weeks before the general election some very suspicious newspaper errors appeared that cast me in a rather negative light. As I left Bisbee for Phoenix after delivering a speech, the local paper ran a story that said, "Raúl Castro had been killed." Actually, an American diplomat in Guatemala had been murdered, and the headlines mistakenly named me as the diplomat that had been assassinated. That night I stayed at a Phoenix hotel next to the *Arizona Republic*, where I intended to conduct an interview the next morning. I purchased a late edition of the daily, and on the front page was a picture of Fidel Castro with a cutline that read "Running for governor of Arizona." The stunt infuriated me, but oftentimes politics, especially in Phoenix at that time, was an unfair endeavor.[17]

On election day, November 3, 1970, Williams defeated me by a mere 7,406 votes out of 410,878 cast (50.9 percent to 49.1 percent). Governor Williams beat me in Maricopa County, 120,608 to 94,838, and I took my home county, Pima, 55,245 to 32,750. It was the closest gubernatorial election in twenty years, and the encouraging results crystallized my resolve to try again.[18]

*Arizona Republic* columnist Walter Meek wrote about the 1970 campaign: "Stripped to its essentials, the governor's race was mainly a matter of personal credentials and whether the voters were in the mood for a change. It was only a small margin of voters who were not in the mood for change. The 1970 election was a very close loss because of slim margins in the rural Arizona counties. That year the Democratic Party lost all of its races except one, the secretary of state position won by Wesley Bolin. The cliffhanger gubernatorial race, therefore, showed Castro to be a very significant challenger." Bernie Wynn, the respected political reporter who wrote the "One Man's Opinion" column for the *Arizona Republic* added: "We believe that Castro has a great future in the Democratic Party and should exercise his prerogatives as titular leader to help rebuild Democratic fortunes."[19]

Shortly after the election I ran into an old friend from law school, Henry Zipf, who asked about my future plans. I said I planned to practice law, and he suggested I join him and a few others. So for the next three years I practiced law, saved money, and planned my next run for governor. I decided to start early in both organizing and fundraising for the 1974 elections. In early 1973 I started the process of seeking out a campaign chairman.[20] Dennis DeConcini, the new chairman of the Pima County Democratic Party and sitting Pima County attorney, who also harbored ambitions for statewide office, accepted my offer. Dennis' father, Evo, a former Arizona Supreme Court judge, state party chair, and party elder, along with fundraiser and businessman Sam Sneller, also joined the campaign's inner circle. With that well-connected southern Arizona group, the money began flowing into our campaign coffers.[21]

At a gathering of Casa Grande business leaders at their local Elks Lodge in March 1973, I signaled my intentions for the next year's elections. "There's more opportunity in the United States today than there was sixty-one years ago," and I said that I planned to retire in Arizona when the time came. I finished my patriotic speech in ten minutes and the question and answer session that followed enabled me to discuss my future plans. One local lawyer asked if I considered seeking the governorship in the next election, and I replied, "I will definitely be running in '74." I touched on the fuel shortage crisis, President Nixon's price wage and freeze, and how Governor Williams sought the wrong solutions for inflation and environmental pollution. I injected federal policy into the mix of challenges and potential solutions that our state faced.[22]

As I prepared for this second campaign for governor, I knew that Eugene Pulliam could greatly affect my chances for success. In my 1970 electoral effort, Pulliam refused to see me or cover my campaign in a meaningful way in either of his newspapers, the *Arizona Republic* or the *Phoenix Gazette*, which were powerful and conservative publications that favored Republican candidates with little variation. Yet early in the 1974 race I received a phone call from the inveterate conservative publisher while I was delivering a speech in St. Johns, Arizona.[23] "Judge Castro," he said, "I'm Eugene Pulliam, and I am hosting a luncheon tomorrow in honor of former Texas governor John Connally, who was wounded in the Kennedy assassination. I really want you there," he added, "and I hope you can come."

My response: "I will be there."

I had never met Pulliam, so I arrived early and asked someone to point out the publisher as soon as he entered the room. "That's him," he said, pointing to the man pushing Governor Connally's wheelchair. I introduced myself:

"Mr. Pulliam, I'm Raúl Castro."

"Oh, wonderful!" he replied. "I want you to meet Governor Connally. Governor, I want you to meet my good friend, Judge Raúl Castro, from Tucson." He acted like he had known me my whole life and we were good friends. The room was full of people from the Republican establishment, including the "Phoenix Forty," a group of self-appointed stewards of the economy. Governor Williams presided as the press snapped pictures and took notes. The luncheon started and Pulliam approached the microphone and introduced a host of dignitaries. Then he announced, "Governor Williams, look, I want to be sure that I'm not losing my mind, I'm getting old, but I don't want to forget to introduce an old friend of mine from Tucson, Judge Raúl Castro." I stood up to tepid applause. An hour into the luncheon, Pulliam stood at the microphone and introduced me again. Everyone assumed he planned to endorse me, so after the luncheon all of the Phoenix Republicans, who nearly sat on their hands when I was first introduced, lined up to shake my hand.

Later during the general election, Pulliam called me to his office and said that he would not endorse me nor would he support the Republican candidate, his distant relative from Indiana. I thanked him and said, "That's all I ask, Mr. Pulliam. It couldn't be any fairer than that." I never saw him again, and he kept his word; I was thankful and admired him for staying true to his promise.[24]

With the assistance of my campaign chairman, Dennis DeConcini, I kicked off my second campaign for the Democratic nomination for governor on March 16, 1974, with a dinner for 900 people at the elegant Mountain Shadows Resort in Paradise Valley, Arizona. Jack Ross, who ran in 1970, was the only announced Democratic primary candidate at the time, and I knew he had a burning desire to win the nomination. I told my audience that fairness and justice were the hallmarks of my campaign, and 1974, with the Watergate scandal and other problems plaguing the Republicans, would be a Democratic year.[25]

Immediately after the Mountain Shadows fundraiser, Jack Williams announced he would not run for another term as governor. "Many years ago," he stated, "I decided that two terms were sufficient for holding the mayoralty of Phoenix, and it seems eight years should be a limitation on this job, and I'm acting accordingly. I have no desire to be a candidate for reelection." He added that he had planned to withhold his announcement until adjournment of the legislature in April or May, but "in order not to impede the plans of those who have been loyal to me, I have decided to advance the date of my announcement regarding my candidacy." This was good news for another former Phoenix mayor Milton Graham, the only Republican who had announced his candidacy for governor. Waiting in the wings was Russell Williams, no relation to the retiring governor, who had resigned from the Arizona Corporation Commission in 1973 to clear a path for the GOP nomination. He issued a statement in regard to the governor's impending retirement: "I am extremely pleased."[26]

Ultimately, two other candidates, Dave Moss, a northern Arizona businessman and political gadfly, and Walter H. "Denver" Caudill, a golf professional at the Tubac Valley Country Club, entered the Democratic primary.[27] The Republican field also grew crowded as Russell Williams, Evan Mecham, William Jacquin, and John Driggs, joined Milton Graham in the primary. As we headed toward the primary election on September 10, I focused my attention on the Republican field and began cultivating the Navajo Nation in northern Arizona, a voting bloc often neglected by Republican candidates. I won the primary, going away with 114,118 votes to Ross' 30,059, Moss' 19,308, and Caudill's 5,773. On the Republican side, Williams' 51,997 votes outpaced Mecham's 29,704, Jacquin's 26,851, Driggs's 23,329, and Graham's 15,438. I squared off against Russ Williams in the 1974 general election for governor of Arizona.[28]

Over the next eight weeks I traveled to every corner of the state and spent much time on the various Indian reservations, especially the voter-rich Navajos, thinking they might be the difference in the outcome of the election. The press described me as a dedicated Democrat and a "scrapper who does best when fighting on the ropes." At the same time pundits labeled me the favorite, which made me a bit uncomfortable. In one profile the *Tucson Daily Citizen* described me as someone who lived on three to four hours of sleep a night and preached that relaxation was for those who had time to relax. My rapid-fire speaking style on the campaign stump prompted Henry Zipf, one of my chief advisors on the campaign, to post a sign in my Tucson headquarters: "Slow down, damn it."

Some observers described me as an "atypical Democrat," one who had forsaken many party principles. I opposed levying a severance tax on Arizona's mines as well as using gasoline taxes for bicycle paths and horse trails; those funds, I told audiences, should be dedicated to constructing roads in rural areas of the state. I supported the death penalty and railed against legalization of marijuana, positions embraced by most Republicans. In most areas, however, I supported Democratic Party principles: I supported the Equal Rights Amendment, local control of public schools, and free textbooks for high school students. In effect, I ran as a conservative Democrat in a right-of-center state.[29]

My opponent, Russell Williams, stated that senator Barry Goldwater's 1964 presidential campaign inspired him to enter politics.[30] A businessman from Indiana who favored less government and lower taxes, the traditional Republican mantra, he moved to Arizona and, due to his connections to the Pulliam family and other Phoenix area power brokers, he was offered an appointment on the Arizona Corporation Commission. In debates he claimed that he helped greatly in changing the commission's tainted reputation. He disdained red tape from Washington and consistently preached states' rights on all public policy issues. We crossed paths numerous times, debated on several occasions, and I found him to be a decent, if uninspiring candidate.[31]

Election day, November 5, 1974, proved historic for Arizona and me. As nearly 70 percent of registered Arizonans voted, I settled in at the Hilton Hotel in downtown Phoenix with my campaign staff and other statewide and congressional candidates. Pima County, my home base, supported me with huge margins, and early in the evening it looked like I would win by a comfortable percentage. Then Maricopa County returns cut into the lead I had built up in Pima and the rural counties. As the night wore on I watched nervously as Williams pulled closer. In fact, at eleven P.M. I had fallen two thousand votes behind, but the Navajo Nation had yet to report. About midnight I learned that I received a majority of about six thousand votes from that important voting bloc; it put me over the top. During the campaign the Republicans ignored them, thinking they would not vote in an off-presidential year election. I traveled to that remote part of northern

Arizona several times and campaigned hard, from Window Rock to Tuba City to Tsaile. I listened to their problems and took their interests to heart. I cared about them, and they voted for me.

Nine hours after the polls closed at seven P.M., in the early morning of November 6, 1974, Williams called me and conceded the election. My razor-thin victory, 276,483 to 272,370—a margin of 4,113 votes in over one-half million cast—made me the first and only Hispanic governor in the history of Arizona. After failing to unseat Governor Williams on my first try, I defeated another Williams on my second attempt for the governor's seat.[32]

A few days after the election, but prior to my assuming office on January 1, 1975, I received a telephone call at my Phoenix hotel. Former governor of Georgia Jimmy Carter identified himself and said he wanted to talk to me. I had never heard of him. I brushed off his request to meet at first, telling him I had to attend the dedication of the Plumbers Union in an hour. He promised it would take only ten minutes, so I relented and agreed to see him. Soon there was a knock on the door and there stood Jimmy Carter and Robert Bergland, who would become secretary of agriculture in the Carter administration. As I dressed for the event, Carter informed me that he was running for president of the United States, and he would like my support. I thought, "Oh my God, another nut!" I terminated the conversation quickly, and later he would laugh and remind me of that first meeting in which I was somewhat dismissive. In the end I supported his campaign for president, traveled the country with him in "Peanut Number One," and grew to know and respect him as an honorable man.[33]

My tenure as governor exposed me to the strengths and limitations of Arizona's constitution, a document crafted in the era of Progressive reform at the beginning of the twentieth century. In short, Arizona's governor, by constitutional design, has limited executive powers. The legislature, I learned quickly, maintained equal or greater power, and programs I championed were often bottled up in the House and Senate. I worked more as an administrator than as a leader in formulating and executing public policy and economic reform. I labored at meeting the state payroll, repairing bridges, paving highways, and providing food and healthcare for state prisoners, since they routinely sued me over food and access to healthcare. The daily duties of the governor's office proved more mundane than my initial impressions.

During my time in the governor's chair I made some, but not all, of the improvements in Arizona I had hoped to accomplish. Unfortunately, the state faced a financial crisis when I took over. Working with the private sector and the legislature, I was able to navigate the ship of state out of choppy fiscal waters. When I took office, the nation and Arizona were in

Official portrait as governor of Arizona.
*Photo courtesy of author.*

the midst of a recession, and I discovered that we had a shortfall of funds to pay state workers. I reduced the executive budget, cutting one million dollars from the previous year despite 10 percent inflation that year, then I called all of the state's leading bank presidents, told them we had a crisis and they needed to be sure that they had enough money in their respective institutions in order for the state to borrow enough to make payroll. With that assistance we avoided an immediate crisis, and shortly thereafter I had every state agency cut its budget by 10 percent. Such draconian measures did little to endear me to state employees, but it was a necessary and responsible course to take.

I convinced President Ford to release impounded federal highway construction funds, which helped reinvigorate our moribund construction industry. In addition, I created the Arizona Commission on the Status of Women and the Office of Affirmative Action in Arizona. To promote trade and tourism, I established the Department of Tourism and expanded the Four Corners Regional Commission to include all Arizona counties. I organized the Border States Regional Commission to deal with US-Mexico border problems, including appointing Pima County attorney Dennis DeConcini as the chief law enforcement official to fight the war on drugs. Finally I set up a national and international trade commission to promote Arizona exports and foreign investments with the Far East, Europe, the Middle East, and Latin America. Clearly my experience outside the US as an ambassador influenced the nature and direction of my years in the governor's chair.

All these initiatives required patience and perseverance, but the most difficult and controversial issue that impacted my tenure in the governor's office involved the Don Bolles murder case, which elicited national and international press coverage and had a serious impact on Pat and me. No amount of patience could wipe away the sadness and trauma of that terrible event. Bolles was an investigative reporter for the *Arizona Republic* and a close personal friend. He visited me at the governor's office each day, and we traveled together to China in an effort to further our international trading goals.

On June 2, 1976, the promise of a tip lured Bolles to the Clarendon Hotel Parking lot at 401 W. Clarendon, where six sticks of dynamite were detonated beneath his compact car. Rescuers arrived, and as the reporter lay dying he whispered "Adamson" and "Emprise." The latter term referred to a New York business that operated in the dog-racing industry in Arizona, which Bolles, in some recent articles, had suggested may be tied to organized crime. Bolles died on June 13, after several amputations failed to save his life, and Phoenix Police promptly arrested John Harvey Adamson, a former tow-truck operator and central Phoenix barfly. Three days later Max Dunlap, a Phoenix contractor, was questioned by lead investigator and homicide detective Jon Sellers, because Dunlap had been observed delivering cash to Adamson.

As the investigation unfolded, a wealthy liquor magnate and southern Arizona rancher Kemper Marley became ensnarled in the investigation. He served as a surrogate father to Dunlap, and many said that he was unhappy with Bolles because of some recent articles critical of his business dealings in the *Arizona Republic*. Prior to Bolles' death, a vacancy had opened on the Arizona State Racing Commission. Senator Paul Fannin, a former Arizona governor called me and recommended Marley for the opening. Senator Fannin touted Marley's knowledge of horses and cattle and thought he would make an outstanding commissioner. Shortly thereafter, Senator Barry Goldwater called and supported Marley for the appointment. Then I received a call from Tom Chauncey, owner of a local television and radio station and spouse of the heiress of the Wrigley chewing gum fortune, and he too urged that I appoint Marley.[34] Others, including cattle and sheep rancher Dwight Patterson and president and CEO of the Valley National Bank, Ray Cowden, lent their names to the growing list. I asked Marley to visit me at the Capitol, told him that Arizona's power elite had recommended him for a seat on the Arizona State Racing Commission and offered him the job. To my surprise he said that he had too many irons in the fire, and he had to refuse my offer. I told him to think about it for ten days and call back. Indeed, he contacted me, said he thought about it and decided to accept the appointment. Soon after his name was linked to the Bolles murder, though he was never charged with a crime.

During the subsequent investigation and criminal cases surrounding the Bolles murder, information emerged that Marley had used the "governor's plane" to fly to Mexico. Some observers assumed that Marley used my plane, but the comment referred to the governor of Sonora, who was Marley's good friend (both men had ranches south of the border in Sonora). Then the press discovered that Marley and his wife and daughter had contributed a total of twenty-five thousand dollars to my election campaign. The public concluded that Marley and I were close friends and associates, though I hardly knew him. The national press, which had made the assassination of one of its own a cause célèbre, followed me for months. It was a very stressful time that was even worse because Bolles had been a friend, and we were profoundly saddened by his death.[35]

On October 20, 1977, two years into my four-year term as gover-

Posing in northern Arizona during my governorship, 1976.
*Photo courtesy of author.*

Pat and I in the governor's office in Phoenix, 1977.
*Photo courtesy of author.*

nor, I resigned the governorship early to take the position of American ambassador to Argentina, which I assumed officially on November 16, 1977. I knew some felt I had betrayed them, but I believed that answering President Carter's call to international service not only advanced the image of Hispanic Americans, but also benefited my constituents. After all, I represented the entire US in the world community and accepting that position raised the significance of my service to Arizona and my country. I was eager to represent the US abroad once again, especially in a country as important as Argentina.

# CHAPTER XI

## AMBASSADOR TO ARGENTINA

During the presidential race of 1976, I campaigned throughout the country for Jimmy Carter, and he suggested that I serve as his Latin American advisor if he won the election. When Carter won and ascended to the presidency on January 20, 1977, he sent word that he wanted me to consider serving as ambassador to Mexico, and at first I said that I would welcome that appointment. On January 27, 1977, I met with Secretary of State Cyrus Vance and informed him that, while I would seriously consider going to Mexico, I did not want to return to Central America, nor would I accept a minor appointment. In February, Florida governor Reubin Askew approached me and said that the governor of Wisconsin, Patrick J. Lucey, who was supposed to be appointed as ambassador to Argentina, could not accept the appointment because his wife's chronic medical condition precluded her from residing too far away from the US. Askew suggested that I take the Argentina post and Lucey serve in Mexico. As I considered the proposition I realized that, since I had many relatives in Mexico who would seek favors, the ambassadorship to Argentina might be more suitable.

By early May 1977 the press had uncovered information about President Carter's plans for me, and on May 5, 1977, political columnist Charles W. Pine wrote, "Rumors of a diplomatic appointment . . . in the very near future were mounting," and "in fact, a reliable source in Washington now tells us that the appointment of Raúl Castro is imminent." The source, according to Pine, said the announcement of my appointment to "some ambassadorship or other position in the Carter administration would take place 'very soon,'" and I had been cleared by the FBI of any involvement with anyone in the Bolles murder case. Pine correctly surmised that my appointment would be to a "Latin American country and not to a State Department post in Washington."[1]

On August 19, 1977, President Carter announced my nomination as ambassador to Argentina. I cancelled a planned visit to the Coconino

THE WHITE HOUSE
WASHINGTON

January 28, 1977

To Governor Raul Castro

I greatly appreciate your having served as
a member of the 1977 Inaugural Committee.
I am especially grateful for the Committee's
success in opening the inauguration to the
people of our country.

You have helped to set an example of what
we Americans can accomplish by sharing
our talents and energies with each other.
Many thanks.

Sincerely,

Jimmy

The Honorable Raul Castro
Governor of Arizona
Phoenix, Arizona  85007

PHOTO 11.01. Thank you letter from president Jimmy Carter.
*Photo courtesy of author.*

County Fair in Flagstaff and prepared to fly to Washington to consult with administration officials.[2] I considered the appointment a promotion, a great honor, and a reflection of the President's confidence in my ability and character. I told reporters that I had mixed emotions because Arizona was my home, and my biggest regret would be that I had to leave Arizona and its wonderful people. I commented that I was proud of my administration, citing a legacy of fiscal responsibility and appointing highly qualified people to key state posts.[3]

The process moved quickly and the Senate Foreign Relations Committee recommended my confirmation as US ambassador to Argentina on

September 19, 1977. I testified before the committee and pledged to do all possible to convince Argentina that President Carter's new human rights policy would be in the national interest. I added that, as a Mexican-born naturalized citizen, I was aware how vital human rights were, and I would work within the limits of diplomacy to convince Argentina of the wisdom of that policy. Republican Senator Barry Goldwater told the committee that he recommended to former President Nixon that he retain me in Bolivia and urged President Carter to utilize my skills in his administration. He even brought up my career as a former boxer, saying that I was undefeated as a professional pugilist. Democratic Congressman Morris Udall testified on my behalf, recalling our years together at the University of Arizona Law School and our early careers in the Pima County attorney's office. After my testimony, I informed the Arizona Congressional delegation that I would not resign the governorship until I took the oath of office as ambassador. By law, Secretary of State Wesley Bolin would assume the governor's chair when I resigned, though I stated that my chief of staff, Dino DeConcini—elder brother to Dennis DeConcini, elected in 1976 as Arizona's junior senator—should enter the governor's race in 1978.[4]

My last official day as governor of Arizona was October 18, 1977, and Secretary of State Bolin, who had served in that position for twenty-six years, was sworn into office as governor. I was sworn in as ambassador to Argentina on November 16, 1977, and Pat and I moved into an elegant French-style palace, which was far more congenial than Argentina's political

---

*The Ambassador*

*of the United States of America*

*and Mrs. Castro*

*request the pleasure of your company*

*at a Champagne Reception*

*on Sunday, March 5, 1978*

*from two until five o'clock in the afternoon*

*6016 East Lincoln Drive*

*Paradise Valley, Arizona*

---

Invitation to champagne reception at our Paradise Valley, Arizona, home, 1978. *Photo courtesy of author.*

atmosphere. The twenty-five room ambassador's residence in Buenos Aires, known as the Palacio Bosch, was built in 1912 by French and Italian artisans and modeled after the Grand Palais, the Petit Palais, and the Trianon at Versailles. It was exquisitely furnished in period style, and our new home was considered one of the finest residences occupied by an American diplomat anywhere in the world. Upon my arrival in Buenos Aires I found a new four-story embassy building two blocks away from my home in the fashionable Palermo District, which replaced a hodgepodge of offices in two buildings in the crowded downtown area three miles away. The security problems restricted my predecessor's lifestyle as Argentina's military government continued to fight leftist guerillas during the transition between US ambassadors. I knew I had to grow used to living with armed guards, and I also realized that US-Argentine relations were somewhat frosty due not only to President Carter's human rights policies but also to his non-nuclear proliferation policies. Both policies were radical departures from previous US administrations.

I also had a sales job of sorts to do. I had to convince Argentines, much as I did with Arizona voters, that a poor man from a Mexican family was worthy of this high position.

Previously the post had been held by two New England Republicans: Bostonian John Davis Lodge, a former movie actor and brother of Henry Cabot Lodge, and Robert C. Hill of New Hampshire, who had graduated from Taft Prep School, studied at Dartmouth, and went on to hold key posts in the United Fruit Company and other large firms between ambassadorial assignments. Some of the upper class Argentines, according to my briefings in Washington, DC, might be more receptive to a "gringo" than a fellow Latin who spoke Spanish with intonations of the Arizona-Mexico border. I was familiar with Argentina, having visited the country while I was ambassador to neighboring Bolivia, and I had received positive press in *La Prensa*, a pro-American mass circulation newspaper and one of Argentina's most influential dailies. But on September 17, 1977, as I was preparing for my ambassadorship in Argentina, an editorial printed in *La Prensa* criticized a remark I made before the Senate Foreign Relations Committee. I told the committee that Argentina should show greater respect for human rights in the best interests of Argentina and the United States. "Such a statement departs from elemental principles and customary standards which govern the conduct of diplomats," *La Prensa* stated. Some interpreted my statement to the Senate committee as critical of the ruling government. Earlier that year the US reduced military aid because the Argentine government, in its efforts to wipe out leftist guerillas, was systematically violating its citizens' rights. With all of these critiques of the Argentine government, I faced serious challenges in my attempts at diplomacy.[5]

Earlier Argentina rejected a reduced US credit for navy arms purchases, and the foreign ministry issued a protest alleging interference in internal affairs. A visit from Terence Todman, the US undersecretary of state for inter-American affairs, appeared to mitigate the situation. President Carter quickly followed this entreaty with a meeting in Washington with President Jorge Videla in October when the Panama Canal Treaty was signed. But Carter's initial plan to bypass Argentina on a world tour that included Venezuela and Brazil was yet another blow to Argentine pride. I lent my voice to others and convinced him to send Secretary of State Vance to Argentina to meet with President Videla and other Argentine leaders. Soon I received word that Vance would arrive in Buenos Aires on November 21, 1977, and I rushed to my new post as soon as I could secure safe passage. I arrived two days before Vance, just in time to host his visit.[6]

My task was further complicated because my predecessor, Ambassador Hill, was very well-liked and maintained popularity in Argentina, especially with the ruling regime, by making speeches critical of Carter's human rights policies. Secretary of State Cyrus Vance's trip to Argentina, Brazil, and Venezuela confirmed just how much the United States reordered its Latin American policies. As noted above, human rights and nuclear non-proliferation replaced Republican foreign policy staples like combating communist subversion in the western hemisphere and concern for the investment climate for US multinational corporations. The moralistic impulse of Carter's policies, I surmised, seemed to have won more favor among the Latin American people than the governments that ruled them. Former President Nixon and Nelson Rockefeller, vice president to Ford, were routinely greeted by hostile mobs when visiting Latin America. Vance's three-day trip, which ended on November 23, attracted only one demonstration: one hundred Argentine women who supported human rights efforts.

Put another way, before Carter the United States was involved in helping Latin American countries improve security procedures through extensive training of police and military operations. The central idea was to enable these nations to track down left-wing guerillas more efficiently. But with the change in US policy under President Carter, these countries were left to their own devices in pursuing criminal elements and political insurgents. The Carter administration's concern lay with the treatment of those detained and whether they received due process. Police equipment, for example, which the US had exported to Latin America in large quantities in the interest of hemispheric security, was now denied to those countries that participated in repression of its citizens. Sales of US weaponry also dropped off substantially, and under Carter there was a substantive redefinition of hemispheric security. He worried less about Cuban exports and subversion and was more concerned about nuclear non-proliferation. Argentina and neighboring country Brazil were Latin America's two most advanced nuclear powers, and Secretary Vance, in the interest of hemispheric security, encouraged both governments to "adopt the strongest possible safeguards" that would not allow either country to develop nuclear weapons.[7] As a result of these policy shifts, Argentine citizens, especially mothers of those detained citizens, came to the embassy and told me hundreds of horror stories. I filed repeated protests with the government. President Carter was very sensitive to human rights violations and sided with the general population against Argentine government human rights violations, so I found myself in a difficult situation.

Buenos Aires is one of the older cities in the western hemisphere. Founded in 1580 in the area that is now the Plaza de Mayo that sits across from Casa Rosa, the executive mansion, it is a global community of great beauty. When I became ambassador in 1977, the population of Buenos Aires was approaching three million. A cosmopolitan city of tree-lined boulevards and stunning architecture influenced by Spanish and Italian artisans as well as other European countries, it maintained a distinctly European flavor.

I arrived at my post in Argentina during "The Dirty War," a period of grievous human rights violations in this advanced Latin American country. "Los desaparecidos," the disappeared ones, amounted to more than thirty thousand people who were allegedly murdered by the military regime. The Dirty War began in late 1975 as an effort by the army to eliminate leftist guerrillas attempting to destabilize the country. It lasted until December of 1983 when the government was overthrown after losing the Falklands War in almost farcical fashion. Those accused of revolutionary ties were picked up in the middle of the night and, with no trial, due process, or notification of family members, were condemned to death—they disappeared, never to be seen or heard from again. Human rights groups were able to document fewer than nine thousand trials, though more than thirty thousand people disappeared. Shortly before I arrived in Buenos Aires in 1977, Juana de Pargament, a mother who lost family in The Dirty War, founded Las Madres de la Plaza de Mayo, a group of mothers demanding information on the whereabouts of their loved ones. To this day they demonstrate once a week in the plaza, demanding justice.[8]

Argentina, which maintained a much larger embassy than El Salvador and Bolivia, stressed its European heritage and downplayed its Latin

American background. I would usually get into my office about seven-thirty or eight A.M., and the first hour and a half was spent reading the daily cable from Washington. Every day each American embassy in the world sent a briefing cable to Washington (to the State Department and the White House), and every morning Washington returned a synopsis and analysis of the previous day's reports. I also had the predictable appointments with embassy staff, American businessmen, and local officials, and I wrote fitness reports—emotional and physical—for all attaché officers. Work at the Argentina embassy never ended at sundown. Evening functions were required. Most considered social events at the embassy enjoyable; but representing the United States government among people one hardly knows, or even dislikes, was not relaxing.

Protocol also played an important role in my work in Argentina, and I erred once in following its strict guidelines. After attending an official function in southern Argentina, my plane flew near the border with Paraguay. I told my pilot that, since we were so close to Paraguay, I wanted to visit American ambassador Robert E. White, in the capital city of Asunción.[9] I visited with my American counterpart in Paraguay, shopped in a couple of stores, then returned to Buenos Aires. Unfortunately those actions were a breach of protocol. Proper protocol required that I first notify the American ambassador in the host company so security could be addressed. I did not do this in this instance.

Later, the Argentine protocol officer notified me that President Alfredo Stroessner, the longtime military and civilian ruler in Paraguay, was in Buenos Aires on a goodwill trip and wanted to meet with me. I greeted him at the embassy, and he said, "Mr. Ambassador, you were in my country a couple weeks ago and you went to the American embassy and to this store and that store, but did not come visit me. I am your friend and want you to come visit me and go fishing and sailing with me." I apologized for this additional breach of protocol but pointed out that it would have been worse to drop in on him without first contacting the American embassy in Paraguay. In any event President Stroessner and I became friends, but his conversation with me served as a reminder that protocol played an important part of any ambassador's work anywhere in the world.[10]

I showed respect to the Argentines by following protocol. They grew annoyed at any sign of disrespect, thus otherwise innocent actions like seating arrangements at a ceremony were extremely important because it symbolized something about seniority and significance. It was important that I follow protocol and show respect since the Argentine people, who considered themselves more European than Latin American, were suspicious of a US ambassador who happened to be a Mexican American. In an effort to gain their trust, I made a point to meet and talk to the general population. They grew to know me, and I won their respect. In time they appreciated the fact that the American ambassador spoke their language, and they soon learned that, besides English and Spanish, I was also fluent in Italian and Portuguese and relatively proficient in German and French. In about three months I overcame the initial negative reaction to my appointment.[11]

As I had in El Salvador and Bolivia, I took to the streets and hinterlands to discover what local citizens thought of the US, their government, and their quality of life. I spoke to cab drivers, waiters, lawyers, teachers, and the general citizenry trying to discern their problems, challenges, joys, and overall happiness. Buenos Aires was a very large city, and if I had not talked to the people on the street I would have insulated myself. The people recognized me since in Latin America the American ambassador was usually the second-most recognizable person after the president.

Security was a serious issue in Argentina. The US Marine security forces were limited to the embassy grounds, sovereign American soil. When I left the embassy, I relied on Argentine security forces. When I walked around Buenos Aires, three or four secret police in plain clothes followed discreetly and, hopefully, inconspicuously behind me. They were close enough that

Receiving the John F. Kennedy Award from Kennedy University in Buenos Aires, Argentina, 1979. *Photo courtesy of author.*

At the ambassador's office in Buenos Aires. *Photo courtesy of author.*

they could come to my rescue if a problem arose. There were other police officers stationed a little further away. When I traveled by car, they used a bulletproof car with bulletproof tires. A taxicab-looking car with police leading the way preceded my car, which had two secret police officers with machine guns. Another police car followed behind our car and all were linked via radio. If I wanted to eat at a restaurant or shop at a store the security detail scoured the location first to ascertain if there were any threats to my safety.[12]

Office security in the embassy was another concern. There was a direct line of sight from the window by my desk to other office buildings about three hundred yards away. At the end of each day, a marine arrived in my office and made sure I did not have any sensitive documents on my desk that could be seen by long range telephoto lenses from the nearby office buildings. They also made periodic sweeps of the building looking for listening devices.[13]

Though American taxpayers pay for most of an ambassador's duties, the government does not cover some significant expenses. An ambassador must pay rent for his residence and domestic help. In Buenos Aires Pat and I had about thirty employees, and we paid a good portion of their wages. I also paid part of the chauffeur's salary. We also covered the cost of all social functions, unless at least 51 percent of the guests were foreigners. So if Pat and I hosted a party, we made sure that at least 51 percent of the guests were not Americans. We kept careful records of all expenditures, and in 1979 I realized that I spent about 75 percent of my personal salary on expenses connected to my job.

HENRY A. KISSINGER

HENRY A. KISSINGER
SUITE 520
1800 K STREET, N. W.
WASHINGTON, D. C. 20006

June 2, 1980

Dear Mr. Ambassador:

I am sorry to hear that you will be stepping down as our Ambassador to Argentina in August but fully understand your desire to return to private life.  You have made a great contribution to furthering relations between Argentina and the United States, and I know you will be missed by both sides.

I, personally, will be sorry to have to forego your matchless hospitality on future trips to Argentina, but I am sure our paths will cross again in Washington or Phoenix.  I will not hesitate to call on you if I need an expert opinion on Latin American matters, and you are exceedingly thoughtful to volunteer.

With every good wish for a most successful and personally rewarding return to your law practice.

Warm regards,

Henry A. Kissinger

The Honorable
Raul H. Castro
American Ambassador
Buenos Aires, Argentina
APO Miami 34034

Letter from Henry Kissinger upon my resignation as ambassador to Argentina, 1980.
*Photo courtesy of author.*

Unlike most American ambassadors, I was not affluent, and I did not have an independent income; it became too expensive for me to be ambassador to Argentina. I had cashed in much of my retirement from my various state and county jobs in Arizona to purchase clothing and other necessities I needed in my position as ambassador, and it became obvious that Pat and I were quickly going broke on the income I had after expenses. In January 1980 I told Pat that I had to quit my job as ambassador and return to Arizona so I could find work as an attorney and make a living. I could no longer afford to be an ambassador from a non-affluent family.

On July 30, 1980, I officially resigned from the foreign service and returned to Arizona, having completed a difficult and dangerous assignment. I wrote President Carter and said that I enjoyed my time in Argentina and was honored that he selected me to one of the most important posts in the ambassadorial corps. I returned to the United States and Arizona anticipating new challenges.

# CHAPTER XII

## CONCLUSION

When Pat and I returned to Arizona in 1980, we bought a home in Paradise Valley in northeast Phoenix, and I practiced law, in an uneventful yet lucrative fashion, in downtown Phoenix. For the next twenty years I enjoyed my practice with good friends and partners Henry Zipf, Al Rogers, and Sidney Marabel. The slower pace and more moderate lifestyle suited Pat and me as we entered our seventies and eighties.

In 2000 we moved to Nogales; a return to a relaxed and quiet life. I continued to practice in the field of international law until I turned ninety, when I finally closed my office and retired. I loved practicing law. It provided me with a good living and great friends, and whenever I have the opportunity I encourage young people to look seriously at law as a profession.

As I survey the historical horizon and assess the various challenges I encountered, I would surmise that fortitude and resolve—others might call it "grit"—served me well. Early in life, when we moved to Pirtleville, I had a sense of determination, and I told myself that I would not be "a dumb Mexican kid." In reality I grew up in a difficult, yet nurturing environment that inured me to the dynamic changes taking place in a rapidly urbanizing civilization that demanded public involvement and participation. Adversity has been my angel, as I have always seen it as something to overcome, not as a roadblock to my success. I was never satisfied with the status quo and always wanted to move ahead, to progress to the next level. If that is "ambition," then it gave me a good life, and I wish it for everyone.

My parents worked hard to provide for my siblings and me, and through seemingly impossible odds I persevered and worked my way through college, law school, and beyond. Fortunately I realized that formal education was the key to achieving one's goals in life. As I embarked on my political and foreign service careers, I met some outstanding public servants and

With former governor Rose Mofford at the inauguration of Arizona governor Janet Napolitano, January 2003. *Photo courtesy of author.*

elected officials including various presidents, senators, congressman and others. My friends and colleagues included Arizona's most distinguished leaders, like Morris and Stewart Udall, Carl Hayden, Barry Goldwater, John Rhodes, and Bruce Babbitt, to name a few. I was also fortunate to meet and counsel with numerous heads of state from all over the world.

I love this country in spite of its imperfections, blemishes, and shortcomings. Together we should constantly strive to make it better and appreciate what we have in this remarkable, hopeful, and productive land of opportunity. In the United States a poor immigrant Mexican child can rise as far as his mental acuity and industriousness will take him. But it takes work—not excuses—hard work. My years in public service were humbling, rewarding, and unforgettable and for that I am thankful. Thank you, America, and all of those kind people who have helped me along the way.

# NOTES

## Introduction

1 Susanne Lassiter to Jack L. August, Jr., November 8, 2007. At age ninety-one, Castro regaled an audience of thirty-five people at the monthly "Teller of Tales" meeting at a Tucson restaurant and triggered the earliest idea to draft this volume. This volume, written in the first person, conveys the hundreds of hours of interviews and transcriptions that now form the Raúl Castro Collection and related archival and manuscript materials at the University of Arizona, Special Collections Department.

2 Little has been published on Raúl Castro but his life and career have been addressed in a variety of scholarly and popular publications. See, for example, Thomas Sheridan, *Arizona: A History* (Tucson: University of Arizona Press, 1995); John Goff, *Arizona Biographical Dictionary* (Cave Creek, AZ: Black Mountain Press, 1991); *Clarin* (Buenos Aires, Argentina) August 20, 1998. After receiving his law degree from the University of Arizona in 1949, Castro's rise was meteoric; deputy county attorney of Pima County (1951-1954), elected Pima County attorney (1954-1958), elected as judge of the Pima County Superior Court (1958-1964); appointed ambassador to El Salvador (1964-1968); appointed ambassador to Bolivia (1968-1969); elected governor of Arizona (elected in 1974 and served until 1977); appointed ambassador to Argentina (1977-1980).

## Chapter 1 Ancestors and Immigrants

1 Raúl Hector Castro, oral history interview with Jack Lassiter, Ben Williams Jr., and Henry Zipf, June 14, 2003, Tucson, Arizona, Raúl Castro Collection (hereinafter Castro Collection), University of Arizona, Department of Special Collections. See also Michael Meyer, Michael Sherman, and Susan Deeds, *The Course of Mexican History* (New York: Oxford University Press, 2006). This volume, which addresses my father's native region, is the best history of Mexico written in the English language that exists. The date of my father's birth was not recorded, but he was born sometime around 1885. Similarly, my mother's birth date was not recorded, but it appears she was born in 1887.

2 Guaymas, formerly known as Heroico Puerto Guaymas de Zaragoza, is a port city located on a small bay on the Gulf of California and at the mouth of the Rio Yaqui, south of the Sonoran capital of Hermosillo.

3 Two readable and informative accounts of Maximilian I and the French Intervention in Mexico are Jaspar Ridley, *Maximilian and Juarez* (Detroit, MI: Phoenix Press, 2001) and R. Conrad Stein, *The Story of Mexico: Benito Juarez and the French Intervention* (Greensboro, NC: Morgan Reynolds Publishing, 2007). Many years later I flew my mother from Guaymas to Santa Rosalía so she could visit her birthplace, and she marveled that it took only an hour, when she recalled it took several days to cross the Gulf of Mexico.

4 The best and most comprehensive analysis of Colonel Greene and his regional impact is C.L. Sonnichsen, *Colonel Greene and the Copper Sky Rocket: The Spectacular Rise and Fall of William Cornell Greene: Copper King, Cattle Baron, and Promoter Extra Ordinaire* (Tucson: University of Arizona Press, 1974). Solid regional accounts of this border area are also contained in Richard Shelton, *Going Back to Bisbee* (Tucson: University of Arizona Press, 1992) and Robert Houston, *Bisbee '17* (Tucson: University of Arizona Press, 1999).

5 For accounts of the strikes against the Four Cs, see Sonnichsen, *Colonel Greene and the Copper Sky Rocket,* 119-144.

6  Because she was female the guards did not search her.

7  Castro oral history interview with Lassiter, Williams Jr., Zipf, Castro Collection, Special Collections, UA.

8  Douglas' "modern" history dates from the late nineteenth century. Originally known as Black Water, due to a dirty water hole at the border, the town formed around the copper industry around 1900-1902. See Will C. Barnes, *Arizona Place Names* (Tucson: University of Arizona Press, 1960), 36.

9  Prior to my father's stint in prison in Hermosillo he worked on the railroad in Arizona Territory for about one year and, as a result my sister was born at Fairbank, a railroad stop in Cochise County. She was American, as was the youngest brother, Ernesto, who was also born in the US

10  My brother, Ernesto, was the second youngest of those who reached adulthood. He was born in Pirtleville on November 5, 1918.

11  The Seventh Street School was later renamed the Sarah Marley School after the woman who was the principal there for years.

12  My father died in 1928, when I was just twelve years old.

13  The literature on the history of the copper industry is extensive. The best treatments on mining, labor, management and regional culture pertinent to this work are Carlos Schwantes, *Vision and Enterprise: Exploring the History of Phelps Dodge Corporation* (Tucson: University of Arizona Press, 2000); Carlos Schwantes, *Bisbee: Urban Outpost on the Frontier* (Tucson: University of Arizona Press, 1992); James Byrkit, *Forging the Copper Collar: Arizona's Labor Management War of 1901-1921* (Tucson: University of Arizona Press, 1982).

14  See also Carlos Cortes, "The Mexican-American Press" in Sally Miller, ed., *The Ethnic Press in the United States: A Historical Analysis and Handbook* (Westport, CT: Greenwood Press, 1987).

15  In Pirtleville, Douglas, and Bisbee my father earned the respect of Anglos and Mexicans alike. If he had not died in his forties he could have done some good things for the area. He was not overly tender or giving to the children, though we knew he loved us. He also drank to excess on occasion, and it was a habit that I disdained and made sure I moderated throughout my long life.

16  Later I found her birth registry book and was amazed at the number of babies she helped bring into the world. It now resides at the University of Arizona in the Castro Collection.

17  Castro, oral history interview, June 21, 2003, Tucson, Arizona, Castro Collection, UA.

18  Later my mother worked with Dr. Hugh Helm who lived in Douglas and developed a healthy respect for my mother's skill sets. Dr. Helm practiced medicine in Nacozari, Sonora, as an employee of the Moctezuma Copper Company, a Mexican subsidiary of Phelps Dodge Mining Company. If a delivery became difficult, he called upon her to assist him. His son, Lloyd, became a superior court judge in Cochise County for many years.

19  Castro oral history interview, Lassiter, Williams, and Zipf, Tucson, August 18, 2004, Castro Collection, UA. Eileen Wright's letter caused me to reflect on bilingual education. My views have surprised many because I have been opposed to the way it has been implemented in Arizona schools in recent years. Mexican American children should speak English well, without an accent, in order to compete for jobs in a capitalist economy.

20  See John Goff, *G. W.P. Hunt and his Arizona* (Pasadena, CA: Socio Technical Publications, 1973); *Douglas Daily Dispatch*, July 5, 1928; Jack L. August, Jr., *Vision in the Desert: Carl Hayden and Hydropolitics in the American Southwest* (Ft. Worth: TCU Press, 1999) especially chapters 2-4; Jack L. August, Jr., "Carl Hayden, Arizona, and the Politics of Water Development in the Southwest," *Pacific Historical Review* 58 (May 1989).

21  *Douglas in Perspective, 2006-2007*, Cochise Community College, Department of Economic Research, 2007. See chapters 2 and 3.

Chapter 2 High School And The World Beyond

1 Actually, few border residents were unaffected by the Great Depression that began in 1929. See Gerald Nash, *The American West in the Twentieth Century: A Short History of an Urban Oasis* (Albuquerque: University of New Mexico Press, 1977) 136-187; U.S. Congress, House Subcommittee of the Committee on Labor, *Hearings on Unemployment in the U.S.*, No. 206, 72nd Cong., 1st sess., 1932 (Washington, D.C.: Government Printing Office, 1932) 98-99; *Douglas Daily Dispatch, Arizona Daily Star, El Diario de Agua Prieta* (Agua Prieta, Sonora).

2 My views on my brothers dropping out of school remain unchanged. In short, they did not have to quit school to go to work; they did not like the discipline it required to study. It was an excuse and I resented it. As a minority working within the broader context of a dominant culture one cannot quit, give up, lose oneself in drink, or blame the system. One has a choice to improve and challenge the status quo.

3 Raul Castro, oral history interview with Jack Lassiter and Ben Williams, July 14, 2005, Tucson, Arizona, Castro Collection, University of Arizona Library, Department of Special Collections.

4 Raul H. Castro, Goldwater Lecture Series Address, transcript, February 13, 2007, Kerr Cultural Center, Scottsdale, Arizona. Talk televised on September 23, 2007, PBS EIGHT, Arizona State University.

5 See Thomas Sheridan, *Arizona: A History* (Tucson: University of Arizona Press, 1995) 109, 329; Rodman Paul, *Mining Frontiers of the Far West* (New York: Holt, Rinhart, and Winston, 1963); *Yavapai Magazine* (February 1918) 4-6.

6 Dr. James Douglas was hired away from a Pennsylvania copper company in 1881 and began working for a trading company known as Phelps Dodge, where he commenced scouring Arizona mining properties. His work led directly to the creation of the Copper Queen Mine, which became one of the top copper-producing mines in the world. He eventually became president of Phelps Dodge. See Schwantes, *Vision and Enterprise*, 11-44. Dr. James Douglas was born in 1837 and died in 1918. Rawhide Jimmy was born in 1867 and died in 1949.

7 The origins of his nickname, "Rawhide Jimmy" have caused significant debate along the border. When I met with him he always wore Levis™ or khakis and an old ragged looking jacket that even I would not have worn. I thought he earned the "rawhide" moniker because of his manner of dress. However, a story persists that originated at the Nacozari Mine that was owned by the Montezuma Copper Company, a subsidiary of Phelps Dodge. One day the Mexican miners were having trouble with the pulley on the windlass that was lifting the ore buckets out of the mine. It kept slipping. So "Rawhide Jimmy" told the workmen to get some rawhide, soak it, and wrap the pulley with it. After the rawhide dried and tightened around the pulley, the problem was eliminated. The Mexican people, in an expression of respect, started calling him "Cuero Crudo," Spanish for "Rawhide." I submit that is the historically accurate account of how he earned his colorful nickname.

8 The standard biography on Lewis Douglas is Robert Paul Browder, *Independent: A Biography of Lewis W. Douglas* (New York: Alfred A. Knopf, 1986); August, *Vision in the Desert*, 122.

9 He occupied an office at the Southern Arizona Bank in downtown Tucson which was l near the county courthouse, where my office was located.

10 I should add parenthetically that I knew and worked with Lewis Douglas' son (Rawhide Jimmy's grandson), James Stewart Douglas, who became president of Southern Arizona Bank. His wife, Mary Peace Douglas, took Spanish from me while I was teaching and attending the University of Arizona College of Law in the late 1940s. Later I became the attorney for the Southern Arizona Bank because of James Douglas' interest in doing business along the border and I helped negotiate a number of business loans in the U.S. and Mexico.

11 Tenth Street in Douglas, Arizona, has been renamed Pan American Avenue. I was one

of the primary movers in the name change because it symbolized the notion of neighborly relations with our sister border city, Agua Prieta.

12  I served as Deputy County Attorney from 1951 to 1954, when I was elected Pima County Attorney, so the rule change was implemented in 1951.

13  Raúl Castro oral history interview with Jack L. August, Jr., September 13, 2007, Nogales, Arizona, Castro Collection, UA Special Collections.

14  I recall that the leading lady was played by Mary Belle Poston, and Virginia Crabtree was the alternate. They were both young Anglo women who became my friends. Castro oral history with August, September 13, 2007.

15  I served on the Pima County Superior Court from 1958-1964 and worked with thousands of juvenile offenders, often seeking out alternatives to incarceration, while at the same time holding them to strict accountability. Often I would divert some of the misguided to educational programs if they seemed relevant in the criminal and judicial process.

16  I kept that letter for years but somehow I misplaced it.

17  Castro interview with August, Nogales, Arizona, September 13, 2007.

Chapter 3 Crucible of Optimism: Higher Education at Arizona State Teachers College in Flagstaff

1  Platt Cline, *They Came to the Mountain: The Story of Flagstaff's Beginnings* (Flagstaff, Arizona: *Northland Press,* 1976); Platt Cline: *Mountain* Town: *Flagstaff's First Century* (Flagstaff, Arizona: *Northland Press,* 1994); Edward Fitzgerald Beale, "Survey of the Wagon Road from Fort Defiance to the Colorado River: Letter from the Secretary of War, transmitting the report of the superintendent of the wagon road," 35 Cong., 1st Sess., House Ex Doc. 77, 1-87; Thomas Sheridan, *Arizona: A History* (Tucson: University of Arizona Press, 1995) 89. The Atlantic and Pacific Railroad arrived in August 1882, which drew those involved in its construction into a small encampment known as Observatory Mesa (or Mars Hill). In 1881, merchants and saloonkeepers set up shop for advance parties of workers who were cutting railroad ties, and by the time the track reached the settlement of two hundred it was already known as "Flagstaff." Beale's Wagon Road, which served as a kind of transportation corridor blueprint for the Atlantic and Pacific Railroad, gave way to Route 66, and ultimately Interstate 40 stretched east-west across this much-traveled area of northern Arizona. Arizona was carved out of the Mexican Cession in 1863, after Beale's survey.

2  Karen Underhill, "I Remember: Depression Era Students at Arizona State Teacher's College," *Journal of Arizona History* (1996) 37, 163-180. Arizona State Teacher's College opened its doors as Northern Arizona Normal School in 1899 with two faculty and an enrollment of 37 and underwent several name changes in its first three decades of existence. In 1945 the school's name changed again to Arizona State College at Flagstaff, and one year later it began offering Master of Arts and Bachelor of Science degrees. On May 1, 1966, the school was granted full university status and changed to its current name of Northern Arizona University.

3  Known as "Walking Woman" in her native language, Ida was an outstanding student and made the honor roll several times.

4  On February 10, 1933, ASTC president Grady Gammage reported to the *Coconino Sun* that the forty animals in the dairy herd, which were a direct result of New Deal programs, saved ASTC $2,606 in the 1931-1932 fiscal year. See *Coconino Sun* (Flagstaff), August 18, 1933, May 12, 1936; September 8, 1939.

5  Dr. Tormey served as president of ASTC from 1933-1944. He stressed small classes, freedom of speech, and the importance of critical thinking over memorization. Incidentally, Dr. Tormey's son Thomas became a law school librarian at the University of Arizona Law School and was an inspiration to me during my years there in the 1940s. Tormey came to ATSC from the University of Iowa and was chosen from among eighty applicants. See *Arizona Daily Sun* (Flagstaff), July 26, 2008.

6  For the best overview of Ft. Huachuca in southern Arizona see Cornelius Smith: *Ft. Huachuca: The Story of a Frontier Post* (Stockton, CA: University Press of the Pacific, 2000)

7  I was actually sworn in as an American citizen after I graduated from college in 1939.

8  Castro interview with Williams, Lassiter, Zipf, Tucson, Arizona.

9  Nacho (Ignacio) became very active in the union and represented them in all negotiations with Phelps Dodge. Although he never went to high school he was intelligent, charismatic, had good common sense and public speaking abilities. The men he represented told me that he negotiated well, and management respected him. I saw a lot of my father in him. He served in the navy during World War II and was involved in thirteen major engagements. He received the Purple Heart and always spoke proudly and fondly about his service to his country. He worked thirty-nine years for Phelps Dodge and retired as a foreman in 1976. He was born November 8, 1912, and he died in 1998 at age eighty-five, leaving me as the last surviving member of this generation of the Castro family.

10  The Border Conference included the Arizona State Teachers College at Flagstaff (now NAU), the University of Arizona, Arizona State Teachers College at Tempe (now ASU), the University of New Mexico, New Mexico State, Texas Tech University, and Texas Western University (now UTEP).

11  Basque sheepherders were an important part of Arizona's pastoral economy, and during the summer they would move their herds to northern Arizona.

12  *Coconino Sun*, March 19, 1939; Cline, *Mountain Campus*, 170-171; 276, 358.


Chapter 4 Return to the Borderlands


1  See Gerald D. Nash, *The American West in the Twentieth Century: A Short History of an Urban Oasis* (Albuquerque: University of New Mexico Press, 1973); Gerald D. Nash, *World War II and the West: Reshaping the Economy* (Lincoln: University of Nebraska Press, 1985); Thomas Sheridan, *Arizona: A History* (Tucson: University of Arizona Press, 1995), 260-262.

2  Nash, *World War II and the West*, passim; Gerald Nash, "Planning for the Postwar City: The Urban West in World War II," *Arizona and the West* 27 [1985], 99-102; Gerald Nash, *The American West Transformed: The Impact of World War II* (Bloomington: Indiana University Press, 1985).

3  Castro oral history interview with Lassiter, Williams, Zipf, Tucson, April 14, 2004.

4  Alfonso died from complications due to shrapnel wounds he received fighting for his country in World War II.

5  I was almost arrested again. Upon arriving in the freight yard in Bakersfield, California, the police raided the train and I was detained. The officer looked at me and said, "You lucky s.o.b., the jail is full. You stay in that car and don't move." I obeyed, and they put those of us in that car on another freight heading to Reno, Nevada.

6  I was in my mid-twenties at this time, but if I arrived home at two or three A.M. my mother would be waiting for me to chastise me about the late hour.

7  See Theresa Williams-Irvin, *Let the Tail Go with the Hide* (Tucson: Mangan Press, 1984).

8  See, for example, *Douglas Daily Dispatch*, June 14, July 22, August 8, 19, 1942; February 7, March 13, 1943.

9  Henry Zipf oral history interview with Jack L. August, Jr., October 18, 2007, Tubac, Arizona. Pusch Ridge, the most prominent feature in the Pusch Ridge Wilderness Area of the Santa Catalina Mounains north of Tucson, rises in elevation over 2,000-5,300 feet at the top of Pusch Peak. Pusch Ridge is in the Coronado National Forest and home to one of the last populations of Desert Bighorn Sheep in Arizona.

10  Castro interview with Lassiter, Williams, Zipf, Tucson, Arizona, October 1, 2003.

11  Sheridan, *Arizona: A History*, 264; Castro, interview with August, Nogales, Arizona, September 13, 2004.

Chapter 5 The Law

1 Castro oral history interview with August, Nogales, Arizona, June 20, 2007

2 Harvill became the fourteenth president of the University of Arizona in 1951, and he served in that capacity for twenty years, until his retirement in 1971.

3 Castro interview with Lasseter, Williams, Zipf, Tucson, Arizona, May 13, 2003.

4 The Hayzel B. Daniels Bar Association of Maricopa County has recently been renamed the Arizona Black Bar Association. Hayzel and I would sit together and study for the bar exam. At midnight we would get hungry, but we had a difficult time finding a place because he was black. There was one restaurant owned by a black couple on Third and Main, and that was the only place we could go to eat.

5 J. Byron McCormick, in 1947, became the thirteenth president of the University of Arizona and served four years in that post. He was succeeded in 1951 by the liberal arts dean, James Harvill.

6 My mid-year graduation did not preclude me from taking more courses in the spring of 1949, which I did, while I continued to honor my teaching obligations at the same time.

7 Henry Zipf was in law school before the war and returned after his service in World War II. He graduated in the class of 1947.

8 John Favour returned to Prescott and formed the well-respected firm of Favour and Quail.

Chapter 6 Pima County Attorney

1 Old Pueblo is the common nickname used for Tucson. See, for example, Thomas Sheridan, *Los Tucsonenses: The Mexican Community in Tucson, 1854-1941* (Tucson: University of Arizona Press, 1992); Henry F. Dobyns, *Spanish Colonial Tucson: A Demographic History* (Tucson: University of Arizona Press, 1976); Michael F. Logan, *Desert Cities: The Environmental History of Phoenix and Tucson* (Pittsburgh: University of Pittsburgh Press, 2006).

2 Castro oral history interview with August, July 20, 2007.

3 The girls, Beth and Mary Pat, were a delight, and I remain proud of them. They attended high school in Tucson for a time then graduated from the American School in the city of San Salvador when I was American ambassador to El Salvador. Beth started college at the University of Dallas in Irving, Texas, and then attended Northern Arizona University in Flagstaff. Later, she went to the Design Institute of La Jolla, and she is now a certified interior designer. Later she also attended National University Law School in San Diego and was certified as a paralegal and as a real estate agent in California. She now resides in Rio Rico, Arizona, just south of Tucson, and is a former president of the Nogales-Santa Cruz Chamber of Commerce. She was married to Don Daley Jr. of San Diego and had two children by him: our grandson, Don Daley III, who graduated from Arizona State University and is now a San Diego businessman; and our granddaughter, Ann Marie Woodard, who graduated from San Diego State and now works for her brother in San Diego.

4 Later she became the first female detective in the Pima County sheriff's office under Sheriff Frank Eyman.

5 The son of Italian immigrants, Ettore "Ted" DeGrazia had an illustrious career as an artist, including a solo exhibition of his work at the prestigious Palacio de Bellas Artes in Mexico City, sponsored by mural masters Diego Rivera and Jose Clemente Orozco in 1942. He gained enduring international acclaim when his painting *Los Niños* was chosen as a UNICEF greeting card that sold millions worldwide in 1960. As the value of his original artwork soared, his fame and finances flourished. To protest inheritance taxes on works of art, DeGrazia hauled about 100 of his paintings on horseback to the Superstition Mountains near Phoenix and set them ablaze in 1976. This infamous event was reported in such publications as the *Wall Street Journal* and *People* magazine, becoming part of DeGrazia's legend before his death in 1982.

6 Word soon got out, and stories ran that Raúl Castro "got stuck in his bathtub."

7 These eventful four years in the mid-1950s transformed my career. I married, took seriously

my public charge to be the best prosecuting attorney I could be, and I began to grow interested in Democratic Party politics. My sincere interest began in 1952 as I observed the beginnings of a political sea change in Arizona as Ernest McFarland, the junior senator from Arizona, ran unopposed in the 1952 primary and seemed assured of election to a third term. He squared off against his Republican challenger, Barry Goldwater, a nice young man who was heir to the Goldwater department store and a Phoenix city councilman. Few people, including the punditry, gave Goldwater a chance, and I assumed, like others, that McFarland would cruise to victory. Goldwater pulled a stunning upset in 1952, and thus began Arizona's inexorable tilt to the political right, which was most evident in the election of Evan Mecham as governor in 1986.

8  *Tucson Daily Citizen*, May 3, 1954 describes Udall's plans to step down from the Pima County attorney's office and run for Pima County Superior Court judge.

9  See also, Donald Carson, *Mo: The Life and Times of Morris K. Udall* (Tucson: University of Arizona Press, 2001) and Morris K. Udall, *Too Funny to be President* (New York: Henry Holt & Co., 1987).

10  *Tucson Daily Citizen*, April 30, 1954.

11  *Arizona Daily Star*, November 3, 1954, *Tucson Daily Citizen*, November 3, 1954.

12  I had ten deputy county attorneys, so it was a small office. During my two terms I worked with Bob Stubbs, Paul Rees, Marvin Cohen, Pete Rubi, Mary Anne Reiman (who later married Bill Richey), Stella Rosenberg, Selma Paul (who later married Jack Marks), Lyle Allan, Frances Wallace, Dick Grand, Whitey Neubauer, and my chief deputy Bud Rogge. I did not have an administrative assistant, so in addition to all of my courtroom duties, I handled press relations, personnel matters, and lobbied the board of supervisors for money. During my four years in that office I worked with one outstanding investigator, Charles Coates.

13  Castro oral history interview with Williams, Lassiter, and Zipf, October 22, 2003, Tucson, Arizona.

14  See Barbara Ann Atwood, *A Courtroom of Her Own: The Life and Work of Judge Mary Ann Richey* (Durham, NC: Carolina Academic Press, 1998). Mary Anne Reiman Richey, a pilot in the Women Air Service Patrol, the lone female in her 1951 graduating class at the University of Arizona law school, prosecutor, state court judge, and federal district court judge. Judge Richey was Gerald Ford's only woman appointment; she was appointed to the bench in 1976 and held this position until her death in 1983.

15  See Dennis DeConcini and Jack L. August, Jr., *Senator Dennis DeConcini: From the Center of the Aisle* (Tucson: University of Arizona Press, 2006), 37-48.

Chapter 7 Superior Court Judge

1  The body of literature on Progressive reform in the United States is extensive, but three sound treatments are Robert Wiebe, *The Search for Order, 1877-1920* rev. ed. (New York: Hill & Wang, 1996); Robert Wiebe, *Businessmen and Reform: A Study of the Progressive Movement* (Chicago: Ivan R. Dee, 1989); and Samuel P. Hays, *Conservation and the Gospel of Efficiency: The Progressive Conservation Movement, 1890-1920* (Cambridge: Harvard University Press, 1959).

2  Sheridan, *Arizona: A History*, 175-176;  Howard Roberts Lamar, *The Far Southwest: A Territorial History, 1846-1912* (New Haven: Yale University Press, 1967)

3  By the second half of the twentieth century, with the state's rapid increase in population, running for the bench had become an onerous burden. Many judges expressed regret that they needed to raise money for campaigns, and they spent enormous amounts of time courting votes, especially with two-year terms. Energy and time were spent on issues outside the performance of judicial duties. Abuse—or the appearance of abuse of power—in connection with campaign contributions left many citizens with perceptions of corruption.  In 1974 the voters of Arizona apparently agreed that these were serious shortcomings in the system, and they approved changes in the constitution to have judges appointed from a list of candidates submitted to the governor by the merit selection committee rather than popular election. Arizona is one of

twenty-four states that use merit selection for the choosing of appellate and general jurisdiction judges. The remaining states use some variation of gubernatorial and legislative appointment, or elections. In Arizona's system voters elect judges for limited jurisdiction courts and general jurisdiction courts in counties with less than 250,000 people (all counties except Maricopa and Pima). When vacancies occur in the Maricopa and Pima County Superior Courts and the Arizona appellate courts, constitutionally designated commissions evaluate a pool of applicants and forward at least three recommendations to the governor. No more than two of the three applicants recommended, or 60 percent of applicants, can be from the same political party. The governor then appoints one of the recommended applicants. Each commission—the Commission on Appellate Court Appointments, the Maricopa County Commission on Trial Court Appointments, and the Pima County Commission on Trial Court Appointments—has sixteen members comprised of ten non-attorneys, five attorneys, and the chief justice, who serves as the voting chairperson of the appellate court commission. Other designated justices chair the trial court commissions. Voters only reformed the system once, in 1992, when they expanded the commission membership and required the commissions take public testimony and vote in public. Though billed as non-political, the commissions are political like any governmental entity. County supervisors appoint selection committees to recommend non-lawyer, trial court commission candidates and then send recommendations to the governor. The governor appoints the selection committee to recommend non-lawyer, appellate court commission candidates. The selection committee then forwards their recommendations to the governor. The board of governors of the State Bar of Arizona nominates the attorney members of all three commissions to the governor. The governor appoints all members with the confirmation of the Senate. Thus, appointments to the commission are political appointments with political strings attached. Commissioners have party designations attached to their names just as applicants do. Other members of the commissions, sitting judges, and other contacts in the legal community lobby commissioners. Although opponents of judicial reform continue to rail against election of judges, there are many potential reforms that could bring more accountability to the judiciary.

4  *Tucson Daily Citizen*, October 15, 1958.

5  *Tucson Daily Citizen*, October 15, 16, 1958; *Arizona Daily Star*, October 16, 1958.

6  *Tucson Daily Citizen*, November 3, 1958.

7  *Tucson Daily Citizen*, November 5, 1958, January 9, 1959; *Arizona Daily Star*, November 5, 1958. Though I beat Robert Roylston in the election, Governor Paul Fannin almost swore him in as a judge before me because he selected him to fill Robert Tuller's position, which became vacant due to his retirement. Roylston was sworn in on January 8, 1958. The judges in Pima County at the time were Lee Garrett, who was presiding (served 1947-1976), Herb Krucker who was assignments judge (1954-1965), Robert Tuller (1951-1959) and John Molloy (1957-1965). And I became the fifth judge, a new division, in January 1959. The judges who later came on the bench during my period were Richard Roylston (1963-1985), Alice Truman (1963-1992), Mary Anne Reiman Richey (1964-1976) and William Frey (1964-1970).

8  Castro interview with August, May 14, 2007, Nogales, Arizona. I ran again in 1960 and 1962. After finishing my first term as judge I ran for reelection, and I remember two things from the second election. First, I met Lyndon Johnson. The Democrats had a campaign rally in Armory Park, and since I was running for reelection as judge, and he was the vice presidential candidate in 1960, he showed up to support Democratic candidates. I was struck by his height and enormous ears. The second memorable aspect of that election was that there were three judge positions open, and there were four of us running for them. The top three vote-getters would win. One of the candidates complained about the names being listed alphabetically. So after that they started to rotate the names, instead of putting them on the ballot in alphabetical order. I won reelection easily in 1960 and 1962.

9  Locals referred to the juvenile detention center as "Mother Higgins," and it served as the county juvenile detention center until 1968, when the current facility was constructed on Ajo Way.

10  *In Re Gault* 387 U.S. 1 (1967). Over forty years ago, the US Supreme Court declared that

all children accused of delinquent acts have the rights to counsel in the proceedings against them.
11 *Tucson Daily Citizen*, September 23, 1958. Pat began "El Milagro Pony Farm" at the River Road property in 1953 and competed successfully in many shows.
12 Jack L. August Jr., "Old Arizona and the New Conservative Agenda: The Hayden versus Mecham U.S. Senate Campaign of 1962," *Journal of Arizona History* 41, 4 (Winter 2000) 385-413.
13 Paul Kleppner, "Politics Without Parties: The Western States, 1900-1984," in Gerald Nash and Richard Etulain, eds., *The Twentieth Century West: Historical Interpretations* (Albuquerque: University of New Mexico Press, 1989) 295.

Chapter 8 Ambassador to El Salvador and LBJ

1 Fannin served two terms as US Senator, from 1965–1971 and from 1971–1977. For information on Arizona Senator Carl Hayden see Jack L. August Jr., *Vision in the Desert: Carl Hayden and Hydropolitics in the American Southwest* (Ft. Worth: TCU Press, 1999).
2 *Eureka Humboldt Gazette*, October 5, 1964; *Arizona Republic*, October 5, 1964. Wayne Morse was an interesting political figure; he was elected as a Republican to the United States Senate in 1944; reelected in 1950; reelected as a Democrat in 1956 and again in 1962, thus serving from January 3, 1945, to January 3, 1969. He was unsuccessful in his reelection effort in 1968.
3 *Tucson Daily Citizen*, October 5, 1964. I also had to resign my Fifth District Superior Court seat effective October 24, 1964, and left the next day for US Foreign Service Protocol School in Washington, DC.
4 *New York Times*, May 4, 5, 1965; *Los Angeles Times*, May 4, 5, 1965; *Phoenix Gazette*, May 5, 1965; *Arizona Republic*, May 5, 1965; *Salt Lake City Tribune*, May 5, 1965. See also, Cinna Lomnitz and Rudolph Schultz, "The San Salvador Earthquake of May 3, 1963," *Seismological Society of America Bulletin*, 56, 2 (April 1966) 561–575. According to scholars who studied this earthquake, it was preceded by a low seismic swarm of three months duration. The main shock—the one that woke us early in the morning—was destructive in a densely populated area and not more than fifteen kilometers in radius. The same area was damaged in 1576, 1659, 1798, 1839, 1854, 1873, 1880, 1917, and 1919.
5 Pat Castro interview with Williams, Lassiter, Zipf, October 14, 2003, Tucson, Arizona. Another aspect of our stay in El Salvador was that the girls attended the American School with many of the children of the "fourteen families," who were the leading families in the country. After we returned to the US there was a revolution, and many of the children that Beth and Mary Pat went to school with were killed or kidnapped. The best book on this event is Robert Armstrong and Janet Shenk, *El Salvador: the Face of Revolution* (Boston: South End Press, 1982).
6 For a brief discussion of President Johnson's Latin American policy see Frank Costigliola, "Promise of Progress: U.S. Relations with Latin America During the Administration of Lyndon B. Johnson," in Warren I. Cohen and Nancy Berkopf Tucker (eds.), *Lyndon Johnson Confronts the World: American Foreign Policy, 1963-1968* (New York: Cambridge University Press, 1994), chapter 4; for his Central American policies see Thomas M. Leonard, *Central America and the United States: The Search for Stability* (Athens: University of Georgia Press, 1991), chapter 8; and for the military assistance programs see U.S. Congress, House Committee on Foreign Affairs, Inter-American Relations, 92nd Congress, 2nd sess.
7 Michael Bomba, "The Effects of International Trade on Sovereignty: The Case of the Central American Common Market" (University of Texas, Doctoral Dissertation, 2003) 99–135; Stephen G. Rabe, "The Johnson Doctrine," *Presidential Studies Quarterly* 36, 1, 48–58. Shortly after American troops landed in the Dominican Republic in May 1965, President Johnson declared his so–called "Johnson Policy," which stated that the United States would never permit a communist regime in the western hemisphere.
8 President Lyndon B. Johnson received a warm welcome upon his arrival at San Salvador's Ilopongo Airport at 9:00 A.M. Saturday, July 7, 1968. Five Central American presidents were there to greet him, and, aside from the estimated two thousand "communist" students who hurled

paint and eggs at his car and held up anti-Vietnam War placards, the motorcade to the Intercontinental Hotel in downtown San Salvador was lined with thousands of well wishers. Before the day was over, Johnson held a two–hour working session with his colleagues, and at its conclusion he announced a $65 million aid package for the region. By the time Johnson returned to the United States on the evening of July 9, he touched down in the capitals (except Honduras, where he stopped at San Pedro Sula) of each Central American country, where he was received equally well. Overwhelmingly, Central American and US newspapers applauded the trip as a resounding success, but in reality there were mixed outcomes.

9  United States National Archives, College Park, Maryland, Record Group 59, Executive Secretariat, Conference File 1966–1972, Lot 69 D182, Box 474, "Scope Paper," June 29, 1968. Hereafter referred to as USNA, followed by RG Number and File Name. For the Trejos visit see: Lyndon Baines Johnson Library, Austin, Texas, The Papers of Lyndon Baines Johnson, National Security File, Country Files, Box 15, Costa Rica, Folder: President Trejos Fernández Visit. Hereafter referred to as LBJ Library, Johnson Papers, followed by box number, file title and folder.

10  Thomas M. Leonard, "Meeting in San Salvador: President Lyndon Baines Johnson and the 1968 Central American Summit Conference," *Journal of Third World Studies* (Fall 2006) 14. Central America fit that need, a place that Mann found to be "traditionally... most sympathetic to us." Rostow did not agree with this observation. He believed that Mann was "out of touch with public reactions in Latin America to recent events in the United States."

11  LBJ Library, Johnson Papers, NSF File, Box 23, Folder: President's Trip to Hemisfair and Central America, July 1968, State Department Circular Telegrams to Central American Embassies, June 4, 24, and 25, 1968; Box 23, Folder: Memos and Miscellaneous, Part 2 of 2, Rostow memos to Johnson, June 4, 7, 13, and 17, 1968. The other Central American capitals were dismissed for various reasons: San José because it had been the location of the Kennedy Central American Summit in 1963; Tegucigalpa and Managua for inadequate hotel accommodations; and Guatemala for security considerations. By the time Johnson decided upon his visit, the Central American presidents had agreed to postpone their meeting for another year.

12  Later the organization was integrated into the larger and more powerful Organization of American States.

13  Hope Somoza Debalye was an American from Miami.

14  As it turned out, I picked up Somoza at the airport and took him to the Catholic church.

15  See *New York Times*, March 5, 6, 1964; *Los Angeles Times*, July 6, 7, 8, 1964.

16  On the downside, El Salvador remained an agriculturally based country, dependent upon coffee exports. It also suffered from an unequal distribution of wealth and a high population density (four hundred people per square mile). The country hoped to capitalize on its central location within the Central American Common Market, its relatively well–developed infrastructure, and an alert, aggressive entrepreneurial class. The Agency for International Development (AID) conducted a variety of programs within the country. In agriculture it offered planning, marketing, supervised credit, land reform, and research and extension projects. In the recent past AID had supported a small industrial development program. In education AID provided for curriculum revision, teacher training, and introduction to instructional television in junior high and elementary schools. AID also provided assistance in fighting malaria and education in family planning.

17  *New York Times*, July 6, 7, 8, 1964; *Port Arthur News* (Port Arthur, Texas), July 6, 1964.

18  Castro interview with August, November 4, 2006, Nogales, Arizona; *Port Arthur News*, July 6, 1964.

19  Castro interview with August, November 4, 2006, Nogales, Arizona.

20  About 2000 youths assembled amid the otherwise enthusiastic, but paid, crowd, and a few splatters of red paint bombs hit the limousine while two eggs hit a press photographer's car. The national guard general, whom I delivered the $6,000 to create a favorable crowd, commented to the press about the protesters: "They are not Communists, just students. Look at the US, they are doing the same thing these days." See *Port Arthur News*, July 6, 1968.

21      Castro interview with August, November 4, 2006, Nogales, Arizona.

22      Ibid.

23      Several books describe and interpret President Johnson's complex personality. See Robert Caro, *The Path to Power: The Years of Lyndon Johnson*, Vol. 1 (New York: Vintage, 1990); Robert Caro, *Means of Ascent: The Years of Lyndon Johnson*, Vol. 2 (New York: Vintage, 1991); Robert Caro, *Master of the Senate: The Years of the Senate* , Vol. 3 (New York: Vintage, 2005); Doris Kearns Goodwin, *Lyndon Johnson and the American Dream* (New York: St. Martin's, 1991).

Chapter 9 Ambassador to Bolivia

1  *Tucson Daily Citizen*, July 15, 1968. The White House press release, picked up by the Associated Press and reprinted throughout the country, read, "The President's selection of Castro for the new position was announced today, one week after Johnson wound up his visit to El Salvador for talks with Central American presidents....Castro, a 1939 graduate of what now is Northern Arizona University at Flagstaff, received his law degree from the University of Arizona in 1949. Last year an honorary doctoral degree was conferred upon him by NAU. He and his wife, Patricia, have two daughters." See also, *El Paso Herald*, July 15, 1968; *Arizona Daily Star* (Tucson) July 15, 1968; *Arizona Republic,* July 15, 1968.

2  *Yuma Daily Sun*, July 15, 1968.

3  *Tucson Daily Citizen*, August 22, 1968.

4  The best recent account on Bolivia is John Crabtree and Laurence Whitehead eds., *Untold Tensions: Bolivia Past and Present* (Pittsburgh: University of Pittsburgh Press, 2008).

5  Laghi would later serve as ambassador to Argentina when I served there during the Carter administration. Thereafter he was the Vatican's ambassador to the United States.

6  In 1964, Paz Estenssoro, who had been elected to his second term as president of Bolivia four years earlier, had the Bolivian Constitution amended in order to be allowed to run for consecutive reelection, feeling that only he had the standing to keep the crumbling MNR together. Traditionally, attempts such as these, known as *prorroguismo*, had been condemned by the Bolivian political elites. This was no exception, and Paz Estenssoro 's controversial move would soon prove to be his undoing. Paz Estenssoro surprisingly chose General Barrientos as his running mate in that year's election, and in August of 1964 the two were sworn into office. Just three months later, Barrientos, together with army commander Alfredo Ovando overthrew Paz Estenssoro in a violent coup d'état and installed himself as co–president in a junta alongside General Ovando. See also *Time Magazine*, August 19, 1966.

7  *New York Times*, May 23, 24, 1965; *Los Angeles Times*, May 23, 1965.

8  See Jon Lee Anderson, *Che Guevara: A Revolutionary Life* (New York: Grove/Atlantic Monthly Press, 1997).

9  Castro interview with August, November 4, 2006, Nogales, Arizona.

10  *New York Times*, May 6, 1969; *Sheboygan Journal*, May 6, 1969; *Los Angeles Times,* May 6, 1969.

11  Castro interview with August, November 4, 2006, Nogales, Arizona.

12  "Rockefeller's Tour: Painful Reappraisal of the Neighbors," *Time Magazine*, July 11, 1969. The New York governor and his party remained at the La Paz Airport and conferred with President Siles and his aides at the air force base adjacent to the commercial airfield.

13  The road to La Paz was susceptible to ambush, and the air currents surrounding the airport were too turbulent so Governor Rockefeller could not travel to La Paz in that fashion. See, for example, *Albuquerque Tribune*, May 31, June 13, 1969; *Arizona Republic*, June 1, 13, 1969.

14  A comprehensive tome on this subject is Gerald Colby with Charlotte Dennett, *Thy Will Be Done: Nelson Rockefeller and Evangelism in the Age of Oil* (New York: Harper Collins, 1995). Rockefeller also wrote a report on his rather difficult mission, Nelson A. Rockefeller, *The Rockefeller Report on the Americas* (Chicago: Quadrangle Books, 1969). See also, *Albuquerque Tribune*, June 4, 1969.

Chapter 10 Governor of Arizona

1  See Robert Alan Goldberg, *Barry Goldwater* (New Haven:Yale University Press, 1995).
2  *Tucson Daily Citizen,* May 1, 2, 28, 1970; *Arizona Republic,* May 2, 1970. Jack Williams served as Mayor of Phoenix from 1956 to 1960 and Governor of Arizona from 1967 to 1975.
3  *Tucson Daily Citizen,* May 28, 1970.
4  *Tucson Daily Citizen,* June 18, 19, 21, 1970; *Arizona Republic,* June 18, 1970; *Yuma Daily Sun,* June 12, 18, 1970.
5  *Tucson Daily Citizen,* June 21, 1970.
6  *Arizona Republic,* June 12, 21, 24, 29, 1970; *Yuma Daily Sun,* June 21, 1970; *Arizona Daily Sun* (Flagstaff) June 19, 20, 24, 1970.
7  *Tucson Daily Citizen,* June 21, 1970. Ross exuded confidence with his horn-rimmed glasses and pencil thin moustache.The thrust of his talks was against Republicans in general and Governor Williams in particular. He contended that Arizona had been a one party state for years and that it was being led down "the primrose path." He mystified many when he told the press that education must be humanized, and Republicans tried to regulate everything with computers.
8  Nader actually seemed to be a pro–business, conservative Democrat. He stated that valuation, population, and overall economic growth had exploded in Chandler during his years as mayor. He pointed out that city property taxes had dropped each of the four years since he had been mayor and claimed Arizona needed a governor with solid business experience. Williams, he said, had been a "don't rock the boat" governor. He stressed economic development as important to the continued growth of Arizona and thought Phoenix received too much attention.
9  *Yuma Daily Sun,* June 21, 1970.
10  *Yuma Daily Sun,* June 21, 1970; *Arizona Republic,* June 21, 1970.
11  *Arizona Republic,* September 6, 1970, *Phoenix Gazette,* September 6, 1970, *Tucson Daily Citizen,* September 6, 1970, *Arizona Daily Sun,* September 6, 1970, *Yuma Daily Sun,* September 6, 1970.
12  *Arizona Republic,* September 9, 1970; *Phoenix Gazette,* September 9, 1970; *Tucson Daily Citizen,* September 9, 1970. In Pima County I won 80 percent of the vote: 20,233 to Ross' 2,826, and Nader's 2,085.
13  Roy Elson oral history interview with Jack L. August, Jr., May 14, 2008, Sonora, Arizona.
14  John L. Myers, ed., *The Arizona Governors: 1912-1990* (Heritage Publishers: Phoenix, 1990).
15  *Yuma Daily Sun,* October 21, 1970; *Tucson Daily Citizen,* October 21, 1970, *Arizona Republic,* October 22, 1970.
16  *Tucson Daily Citizen,* October 2, 1970.
17  Castro interview with August, November 4, 2007, Nogales, Arizona.
18  *Tucson Daily Citizen,* November 6, 1970. I won nine of Arizona's fourteen counties in the gubernatorial election of 1970.
19  *Arizona Republic,* October 6, 10, 16, November 6, 1970.
20  Originally, I asked John Molloy to serve as my campaign chairman, but his law firm indicated they could not spare him for that amount of time.
21  See Dennis DeConcini and Jack L. August, Jr., *Senator Dennis DeConcini: From the Center of the Aisle* (Tucson: University of Arizona Press, 2006).
22  *Casa Grande Daily Dispatch,* March 15, 1973.
23  I was visiting a fellow former judge, Richard Greer, who had served on the Apache County Superior Court; He said he supported me, but that I would not secure the Mormon vote, so I would lose in St. Johns, Holbrook, Safford and other Latter-Day Saints communities.
24  Periodically during the campaign, the managing editor of the *Arizona Republic,* Harold Milks, called and indicated that Pulliam wanted to know the campaign's status. I believe he wanted me to win but could not officially support me because of his family and political ties. He was square with me in the 1974 campaign.
25  *Arizona Republic,* March 17, 1974; *Yuma Daily Sun,* March 17, 1974. *Tucson Daily Citizen,* March 4, 1974. I made my official announcement for candidacy on March 3, 1974.

26 *Arizona Republic,* April 2, 1974; *Tucson Daily Citizen*, March 30, 1974.

27 *Tucson Daily Citizen*, March 19, 1974.

28 *Tucson Daily Citizen*, September 11, 1974, *Arizona Republic*, September 11, 1974. Mecham would be elected governor in 1986. Driggs, like Graham, was a former Phoenix mayor.

29 *Arizona Republic*, September 11, 15, 17, 18, October 1, 4, 18, 1974; *Tucson Daily Citizen*, October 21, 22, 1974; *Phoenix Gazette*, September 22, 25, October 21, 24, 1974.

30 Williams' family owned a chain of gas stations in Indiana, and he expanded the business into Arizona.

31 *Tucson Daily Citizen*, October 21, 1974.

32 My victory broke an eight–year Republican grip on the governorship, and I assumed office with the state senate's Democrats taking command of the upper house of the legislature, 18 to 12, for the first time since 1906, during the territorial period. I "squeezed through," as one reporter put it, by carrying the outer state counties that had a Democratic registration edge. Cesar Chavez and the United Farm Workers actually hurt my candidacy in border areas in Cochise and Yuma counties. Williams claimed that, as a result of the Watergate scandal, Americans across the country were disenchanted with the Republican Party, and this distrust was the main reason for his defeat. Voters, he said, had a different attitude than he maintained, and he suggested that they were "a lot more concerned about Watergate than I expected." *Arizona Republic*, November 6, 7, 1974; *Tucson Daily Citizen*, November 6,7,8, 1974.

33 President Gerald Ford, on the other hand, never remembered my name correctly. He thought I was "Paul Castro" and that I was from New Mexico. I would correct him and say that I was Raúl from Arizona, and he would say, "Oh, right," and apologize. However, without variation, the next time he would see me he would greet me with, "Hi, Paul, how are things in New Mexico?"

34 Chauncey maintained a Scottsdale Arabian horse ranch and devoted much energy in this business endeavor.

35 *Arizona Republic,* June 3, 2001. The Don Bolles saga stretched over nearly two decades. On January 15, 1977, in an agreement with prosecutors, Adamson admitted planting the remote control bomb and plead guilty to second-degree murder. He agreed to cooperate with prosecutors in exchange for a twenty-year, two-month prison sentence. Police arrested Dunlap and James Robison, a Chandler plumber who allegedly helped Adamson by triggering the bomb. The Dunlap and Robison trial began on July 6, 1977. They were charged with first-degree murder. On November 6, 1977, a jury found Dunlap and Robison guilty based on the strength of Adamson's testimony. On January 10, 1978, Dunlap and Robison were sentenced to death. On February 25, 1980, the Arizona Supreme Court overturned the convictions of Dunlap and Robison and ordered a new trial. In June of 1980 the charges against Dunlap and Robison were dismissed and Adamson's original charge was reinstated. He was found guilty and sentenced to death that same year. Over the next ten years, Adamson's death sentence would be overturned, reinstated, overturned again in an appeals court, and brought before the US Supreme Court where the appeals court ruling was left intact. The charges against Dunlap and Robison were reinstated in 1990, and in 1993 Adamson agreed to testify against Dunlap and Robison in return for the reinstatement of his 1977 plea bargain and twenty-year, two month prison sentence. Finally Dunlap was found guilty and sentenced to life in prison in 1993. Robison was acquitted in 1993, but plead guilty to soliciting an act of criminal violence for trying to have Adamson (the chief witness against him) killed and was sentenced to five years in federal prison in 1995. He was released in 1998. On August 12, 1996, Adamson was released from prison and headed into the federal Witness Protection Program, which he would voluntarily leave a few years later.

Chapter 11 Ambassador to Argentina

1 *Gallup Independent*, May 11, 1977; *Arizona Republic*, May 11, 1977. Castro interview with Jack L. August Jr., Tubac, Arizona, October 31, 2008.

2 The Associated Press noted that "the appointment would end months of speculation about the future of Castro, who has been known to be in line for a diplomatic post." *Washington Post*, August 19, 1977; *Hobbs Daily News* (Hobbs, New Mexico), August 21, 1977; *Arizona Daily Sun* (Flagstaff) August 19, 1977.

3 *Arizona Daily Star*, August 19, 1977; *Hobbs Daily News*, August 21, 1977.

4 *Arizona Republic*, September 14, 1977; *Gallup Independent*, September 14, 1977; *Arizona Daily Star*, September 14, 17, 19, 1977.

5 *La Prensa* (Buenos Aires) September 17, 1977. See also Thomas C. Wright, *State Terrorism in Latin America: Chile, Argentina and International Human Rights* (Lanham, Maryland: Rowan & Littlefield Publishing, Inc., 2007), 122-125. This cogent monograph examines the development and resolution of Latin America's human rights crisis of the 1970s and 1980s. Thomas Wright focuses especially on state terrorism in Chile under General Augusto Pinochet (1973-1990) and in Argentina during the Dirty War (1976-1983). He offers a nuanced exploration of the recipro-cal relationship between Argentina and Chile and human rights movements, clearly demonstrat-ing how state terrorism in these countries strengthened the international human rights lobby and how that more powerful lobby ultimately helped bring repressors to justice.

6 *New York Times*, November 21, 22, 23, 25, 1977; *Arizona Republic*, November 24, 1977.

7 Robert A. Strong, *Jimmy Carter and the Making of American Foreign Policy* (Miller Center Series on the American Presidency) (Baton Rouge: Louisiana State University Press, 2000); Douglas Brinkley, *The Unfinished Presidency: Jimmy Carter's Journey Beyond the White House* (New York: Penguin, 1999).

8 David Rock, *Argentina, 1516-1987* (Berkeley: University of California Press, 1987); Max Hastings and Simon Jenkins, *The Battle for the Falklands* (New York: W.W. Norton, 1984); Robert D. Crassander, *Peron and the Enigma of Argentina* (New York: W.W. Norton, 1996).

9 See John T. Woolley and Gerhard Peters, *The American Presidency Project* [online], Santa Barbara; University of California. www.presidency.ucsb.edu.

10 *Washington Post*, August 17, 2006; Hugh M. Hamill, *Caudillos: Dictators in Spanish America* (Norman: University of Oklahoma Press, 1995); Paul H. Lewis, *Paraguay Under Stroessner* (Chapel Hill: University of North Carolina Press, 1980); Carlos R. Miranda, *The Stoessner Era: Authori-tarian Rule in Paraguay* (Bellevue, Tennessee: Westview Press, 1990); Rene Hander Horst, *The Stroessner Regime and Indigenous Resistance in Paraguay* (Gainesville: University of Florida Press, 2007). Stroessner's rise to power began when he objected to President Federico Chávez' plans to arm the national police. Stroessner threw him out of office in a coup d'état on May 4, 1954. After a brief interim presidency by Tomás Romero, Stroessner was the only candidate in a spe-cial election on July eleventh to complete Chávez' term. He was reelected, and in some of his other elections he won by implausibly high margins (well over 80 percent in many cases). He served for thirty-five years.

11 With respect to other protocol matters, the rule at dinners was that the hosts sat at the ends of the table, and the guests sat in descending order according to seniority, with those of lowest seniority at the center of the table. The countries were not seated according to the importance or size of the country (that would start wars), but according to how long that particular ambas-sador had been in that particular country. Within the embassy, there were American military attaché officers assigned to the embassy and other American regular military officers assigned for military functions within the country. If the function was a dinner for a visiting American general, then the regular military officers took priority over military attaché officers, who are considered part of the diplomatic staff. But if the function was diplomatic in nature, then the military attaché officers took priority over regular military officers. Without these rules, snubs

could be imagined and cause problems, particularly among military officers, who lived by the rank structure and its privileges.

12  The same type of security detail followed Pat all around Argentina.

13  Spying was a major preoccupation during my stay in Argentina. At one point, Chile accused me of spying for Argentina. I used to visit a little town called Ushuia, on the southern tip of Argentina, the southernmost town in Latin America. I went there about once a month, and to get there we flew along the Chilean border with Argentina. Chilean military advisors became convinced that I was spying for Argentina. After several candid discussions my travels no longer raised suspicions.

Chapter 12 Conclusion
[No notes]

## BOOKS

Anderson, Jon Lee. *Che Guevara: A Revolutionary Life.* New York: Grove/Atlantic Monthly Press, 1997.

Armstrong, Robert and Shenk, Janet. *El Salvador: The Face of Revolution.* Boston: South End Press, 1982.

Atwood, Barbara: *A Courtroom of Her Own: The Life and Work of Judge Mary Ann Richey.* Durham, NC: Carolina Academic Press, 1998.

August, Jack. *Vision in the Desert: Carl Hayden and Hydropolitics in the American Southwest.* Ft. Worth: TCU Press, 1999.

_____. *Senator Dennis DeConcini: From the Center of the Aisle.* Tucson: University of Arizona Press, 2006.

Barnes, Will C. *Arizona Place Names.* Tucson: University of Arizona, 1960.

Brinkley, Douglas. *The Unfinished Presidency: Jimmy Carter's Journey beyond the White House.* New York: Penguin, 1999.

Browder, Robert Paul. *Independent: A Biography of Lewis W. Douglas.* New York: Alfred A. Knopf, 1986.

Byrkit, James. W. *Forging the Copper Collar: Arizona's Labor Management War of 1901-1921.* Tucson: University of Arizona Press, 1982.

Caro, Robert. *The Path to Power: The Years of Lyndon Johnson.* New York: Vintage, 1990.

_____. *Means of Ascent: The Years of Lyndon Johnson.* New York: Vintage, 1991.

_____. *Master of the Senate: The Years of Lyndon Johnson.* New York: Vintage, 2005.

Carson, Donald. *Mo: The Life and Times of Morris K. Udall.* Tucson: University of Arizona Press, 2001.

Cline, Platt. *They Came to the Mountain: The Story of Flagstaff's Beginnings.* Flagstaff: Northland Publishing, 1976.

_____. *Mountain Town: Flagstaff's First Century.* Flagstaff: Northland Publishing, 1994.

Cohen, Warren and Tucker, Nancy Berkhopf. *Lyndon Johnson Confronts the World: American Foreign Policy, 1963-1968.* New York: Cambridge University Press, 1994.

Crabtree, John and Whitehead, Laurence. *Untold Tensions: Bolivia Past and Present.* Pittsburgh: University of Pittsburgh Press, 2008.

Crassander, Robert. *Peron and the Enigma of Argentina.* New York: W.W. Norton, 1996.

Dobyns, Henry F. *Spanish Colonial Tucson: A Demographic History.* Tucson: University of Arizona Press, 1976.

Farish, Thomas, Edwin. *Arizona History.* Phoenix: Phoenix Manufacturing Company, 1920.

Goff, John P. *George W. P. Hunt and his Arizona.* Pasadena: Socio-Technical Publications, 1973.

Goldberg, Robert Alan. *Barry Goldwater.* New Haven: Yale University Press, 1995.

Goodwin, Doris Kearns. *Lyndon Baines Johnson and the American Dream.* New York: St. Martin's Press, 1991.

Hamill, Hugh M. *Caudillos: Dictators in Spanish America.* Norman: University of Oklahoma Press, 1995.

Hastings, Max and Jenkins, Simon. *The Battle for the Falklands*. New York: W. W. Norton, 1984.

Hays, Samuel P. *Conservation and the Gospel of Efficiency: The Progressive Conservation Movement, 1890-1920*. Cambridge: Harvard University Press, 1949.

Houston, Robert. *Bisbee '17*. Tucson: University of Arizona Press, 1999.

Horst, Horde, Rene. *The Stroessner Regime and Indigenous Resistance in Paraguay*. Gainesville: University of Florida Press, 2007.

Irwin, Theresa Williams. *Let the Tail Go with the Hide*. Tucson: Mangan Press, 1984.

Lamar, Howard, R. *The Far Southwest, 1846-1912: A Territorial History*. New Haven: Yale University Press, 1966.

Leonard, Thomas M. *Central America and the United States: The Search for Stability*. Athens: University of Georgia Press, 1991.

Lewis, Paul. *Paraguay Under Stroessner*. Chapel Hill, NC: University of North Carolina Press, 1980.

Logan, Michael. Desert *Cities: The Environmental History of Phoenix and Tucson*. Pittsburgh: University of Pittsburgh Press, 2006.

Lowitt, Richard. *The New Deal and the West*. Bloomington: University of Indiana Press, 1984.

Luckingham, Bradford. *The Urban Southwest: A Profile History of Albuquerque, El Paso, Phoenix, and Tucson*. El Paso: Texas Western Press, 1982.

Meinig, D. W. *Southwest: Three Peoples in Geographical Change, 1600-1970*. New York: Oxford University Press, 1971.

Miller, Sally ed. *The Ethnic Press in the United States: A Historical Analysis and Handbook*. Westport, CT: Greenwood Press, 1987.

Miranda, Carlos. *The Stroessner Era: Authoritarian Rule in Paraguay*. Bellevue, TN: Westview Press, 1990.

Meyer, Michael. *The Course of Mexican History*. 8th Edition. New York: Oxford University Press, 2006.

Myers, John L. ed. *The Arizona Governors, 1912-1990*. Phoenix: Heritage Publishers, 1990.

Nash, Gerald. The *American West in the Twentieth Century: A Short History of an Urban Oasis*. Albuquerque: University of New Mexico Press, 1973.

_____. *The American West Transformed: The Impact of World War II*. Bloomington: University of Indiana Press, 1985.

_____. *World War II and the West: Reshaping the Economy*. Lincoln: University of Nebraska Press, 1990.

Nash, Gerald and Etulain, Richard. *The Twentieth Century West: Historical Interpretations*. Albuquerque: University of New Mexico Press, 1989.

Paul, Rodman. *Mining Frontiers of the Far West*. New York: Holt, Rinehart, and Winston, 1963.

Pomery, Earl. *The American Far West in the Twentieth Century*. New Haven: Yale University Press, 2008.

Ridley, Jaspar. *Maximilian and Juarez*. Detroit, MI: Phoenix Press, 2001.

Rock, David. *Argentina, 1516-1987*. Berkeley: University of California Press, 1987.

Schwantes, Carlos. *Vision and Enterprise: Exploring the History of Phelps Dodge Corporation*. Tucson: University of Arizona Press, 2000.

_____. *Bisbee: Urban Outpost on the Frontier*. Tucson: University of Arizona Press, 1992.

Shelton, Richard. *Going Back to Bisbee*. Tucson: University of Arizona Press, 1992.

Sheridan, Thomas. *Arizona: A History.* Tucson: University of Arizona Press, 1995.

Sonnichsen, C. L. *Colonel Greene and the Copper Sky Rocket: The Spectacular Rise and Fall of William Cornell Greene, Copper King, Cattle Baron, and Promoter Extra Ordinaire.* Tucson: University of Arizona Press, 1974.

Smith, Cornelius. *Ft. Huachuca: The Story of a Frontier Post.* Stockton: University of Pacific Press, 2000.

Smith, Karen. The *Magnificent Experiment: Building the Salt River Reclamation Project.* Tucson: University of Arizona Press, 1984.

Stein, Conrad R. *The Story of Mexico: Benito Juarez and the French Intervention.* Greensboro, NC: Morgan Reynolds Publishing, 2007.

Strong, Robert A. *Jimmy Carter and the Making of American Foreign Policy.* Baton Rouge: University of Louisiana Press, 2000.

Udall, Morris K. *Too Funny to be President.* New York: Henry Holt & Company, 1987.

Wendland, Michael F. *The Arizona Project.* Kansas City, MO: Sheed Andrews and McMeel, 1977.

Wiebe, Robert. *The Search for Order,* rev. ed. New York: Hill and Wang, 1996.

_____. *Businessmen and Reform: A Study of the Progressive Movement.* Chicago: Ivan R. Dee, 1989.

Wiley, Peter and Gottlieb, Robert. *Empires in the Sun: The Rise of the New American West.* New York: G.P. Putnam and Sons, 1982.

Wright, Thomas C. *State Terrorism in Latin America: Chile, Argentina, and International Human Rights.* Lanham, MD: Rowan and Littlefield Publishing, 2007.

INTERVIEWS

Castro, Raúl. Multiple interviews with co-author, Nogales, Tucson, Arizona 2006-2008.

Castro, Raúl. Multiple interviews with Henry Zipf, Jack Lassiter, and Ben F. Williams, 2004-2006.


JOURNAL ARTICLES

August, Jack, L. "Carl Hayden: Born a Politician." *Journal of Arizona History* 26 (Summer 1985).

_____. "Carl Hayden, Arizona, and the Politics of Water Development in the Southwest, 1923-1928." *Pacific Historical Review* 58 (May 1989).

_____. "A Sterling Young Democrat: Carl Hayden's Road to Congress, 1900-1912." *Journal of Arizona History* 28 (Autumn 1987).

_____. "Carl Hayden's 'Indian Card': Environmental Politics and the San Carlos Reclamation Project." *Journal of Arizona History* 34 (Winter 1993).

_____. "A Vision in the Desert: Charles Trumbull Hayden, Salt River Pioneer." *Journal of Arizona History* 36 (Summer 1995).

Caughey, John. "The Insignificance of the Frontier in American History." *Western Historical Quarterly* 5 (January 1974).

Lamar, Howard R. "Persistent Frontier: The West in the Twentieth Century," *Western Historical Quarterly* 7 (January 1973).

Lamb, Blaine. "A Many Checkered Toga: Arizona Senator Ralph Cameron, 1921-1927," *Arizona and the West 19* (Spring 1977).

Leonard, Thomas, M. "Meeting in San Salvador: President Lyndon Baines Johnson and the 1968 Central American Summit Conference," *Journal of Third World Studies* (Fall 2006).

Lomnitz, Cinna and Schultz, Rudolph. "The San Salvador Earthquake of May 3, 1963," *Seismological Society of American Bulletin*, 56 2 (April 1966).

Nash, Gerald, "Planning for the Postwar City: The Urban West in World War II," *Arizona and the West* 27 (1985).

Rabe, Stephen, "The Johnson Doctrine," *Presidential Studies Quarterly* 36 1 (2006).

Underhill, Karen. "I Remember: The Depression Era Students at Arizona State Teachers College," *Journal of Arizona History* 36 (Summer 1996).

NEWSPAPERS AND PERIODICALS
*Arizona Blade Tribune* (Florence)
*Arizona Daily Star* (Tucson)
*Arizona Daily Sun* (Flagstaff)
*Arizona Republic* (Phoenix)
*Casa Grande Valley Dispatch*
*Daily Courier* (Prescott)
*Douglas Daily Dispatch*
*Gallup Independent*
*La Prensa* (San Antonio, Texas)
*La Voz Del Pueblo* (Phoenix).
*Los Angeles Times*
*New York Times*
*Nogales Daily Herald*
*Time Magazine* (New York)
*Tucson Daily Citizen*
*Washington Post*
*Yuma Daily Sun*

MANUSCRIPT COLLECTIONS
Governor Raúl Castro Papers, 1974-1977. Arizona Department of Library, Archives and Public Records, Phoenix.

The Raúl Castro Collection. Special Collections, University of Arizona Library, Tucson.

The Presidential Papers of Lyndon Baines Johnson. Lyndon Baines Johnson Presidential Library, Austin, Texas.

# INDEX

Acosta, Rosario. *See* Castro, Rosario
Adamson, John Harvey, 93, 121n35
African Americans, 34
Agency for International Development (AID), 60, 118n16
airplane emergencies, 75
Aldridge, Gordon, 42
American Consulate, Agua Prieta, Sonora (Mexico), 29–30, 31
American School, El Salvador, 117n5
Argentina
    ambassadorial appointment and duties, 95, 96–98, 101–102, 103, *104*
    capital cities of, 101
    espionage accusations, 123n13
    lifestyle in, 98–99, 102–105
    political climate in, 101–102
    resignation and letter from Kissinger, 105, *105*
    US foreign policies in, 98, 99–101
Arguedas, Antonio, 74–75
Arizona, history of
    Flagstaff area, 18
    judge appointment procedures, 45, 45n3
    post-Depression growth, 25–26
    radical to conservative political shift, 52
    statehood and constitution, 45–46
    territorial period and federal spending, 25
Arizona Black Bar Association, 114c5n4
Arizona Commission on the Status of Women, 92
Arizona Constitution, 45–46, 91
*Arizona Republic* (newspaper), 85, 87, 88, 93
Arizona State Racing Commission, 93
Arizona State Teachers College (ASTC), 17, 18–19, 21–24
Army National Guard, 20
Arnold, Jack, 41
Arnold, Joe, 46
art education, 23
Askew, Reubin, 96
ASTC (Arizona State Teachers College), 17, 18–19, 21–24
Atkinson, Alfred, 34–35
Atkinson's Hillswicke Blue Boy (horse), 50
Atlantic and Pacific Railroad, 112n1
automobile raffles, 41